The *Girlfriend's* Fabulous Guide to Real Estate

The Woman's Manual to
Buying, Owning and Selling a Home

Christine Denty

 FriesenPress

Suite 300 - 990 Fort St
Victoria, BC, Canada, V8V 3K2
www.friesenpress.com

Copyright © 2016 by Christine Denty
First Edition — 2016

All rights reserved.

No part of this publication may be reproduced in any form, or by any means, electronic or mechanical, including photocopying, recording, or any information browsing, storage, or retrieval system, without permission in writing from FriesenPress.

ISBN
978-1-4602-3268-2 (Hardcover)
978-1-4602-3269-9 (Paperback)
978-1-4602-3270-5 (eBook)

1. *Business & Economics, Real Estate*

Distributed to the trade by The Ingram Book Company

Table of Contents

v • About Christine Denty

vii • Why I Wrote This Book

ix • You Will Survive This, Maybe

xi • Real Estate Truths and Myths

xiii • How to Use This Book

xv • An Overview of Real Estate in Canada

1 • Buying a Home

    Buyer Timeline: • 3
    Financing your Purchase • 5
    Housing Options • 11
    Buyer's Closing Costs • 15
    Carrying Costs • 19
    Home Inspection • 23
    Insurance • 27
    Home buying Scenarios: • 31
    Buying a rental property... • 33
    Buying a Property with Someone Else • 37
    Power of Sales • 39
    Estate Purchase • 41
    Setting up Utilities • 43
    Moving and Packing Tips • 45

47 • Owning a Home

Home Maintenance Plan • 49
Septic Systems • 57
Home Alarms • 59
Home Emergency Kit • 63
Fire Emergency • 75
Pests • 79
How to Deal with Neighbours (Good and Bad) • 83
Taxation and Write-Offs • 85
To Renovate or Not to Renovate • 87

89 • Selling your Home

Seller's Timeline • 91
Knowing the Real Estate Market before Selling your Home • 93
How to Choose a REALTOR® to Sell your Home • 99
How Does Real Estate Commission Work? • 101
Preparing your Home for Sale • 103
Staging your home • 105
Your Open House • 115
Getting an Offer • 117
Seller's Closing Costs • 133

135 • Conclusion

137 • Appendix (Home Inspection)

About Christine Denty

I am a human being; a woman, a mother, a career girl, crusty at times, and sometimes too naïve in certain relations with people. I wish I could leave it at that. I go through difficult life stages just as you do. Sometimes it sucks being human, (I observe as my cat lounges on my bed, staring at nothing, never pondering her next meal or how she will rid her ass of cellulite). But today it doesn't suck being human, and it doesn't suck being a woman. It doesn't suck being a "mature" woman.

This is the last of the writings of my book. I saved doing this chapter for the end. I knew the impression I would have of me would be humbled after writing all the other chapters. But guess what? Far from it. I am far from perfect. VERY far! I survived my second divorce (at only forty one years old!) mostly for MY mistakes, not his. I spend more than I make, I have potty mouth, and I drink too much wine. Ironic how such a misfit could be writing a self-help guide to real estate. But these imperfections I embody are perfect for whom and what I represent. I suspect I may have experience in so many life stages ahead of many of the readers of this book. Not all the good stuff. Mostly the bad. But today, I am fantastic. I finished this. I am an even more accomplished woman today than I was two years ago when I started to write this book. For once I am really proud of myself. I didn't forge this. I did all my research, designed all the charts and pie graphs, came up with all the topics, and finished a book! I, like many, start a lot of projects and never finish. I say that I am "ADD" to justify why I don't finish anything I start. As of today, I will never, ever again excuse my inability to finish something that gives me meaning and hope. It was up to me to deem my self-worth important enough to finish this, and I did.

I was not a writer, I was a REALTOR® – a REALTOR® suffering through her second divorce; scared and feeling defeated. Today I am an author, and a REALTOR®. I won awards the last few years for my property sales. I feel like a woman on fire. I survived my move and the future is beautiful and happy. I understand who we are and what we need to do to preserve our sanity, security, and wealth and the flow of love coming into our lives. I am the modern (yet imperfect) woman, who sees her mistakes as the best thing that could have ever happened to her. *I am Christine Denty.*

not intended to solicit those under contract

This book is dedicated to, and wouldn't be possible without:

My beautiful daughters Francesca and Natalie

My strong and loving mother Louise

My crazy American boy Eric

The LCBO.

Why I Wrote This Book

Don't you love those feminine product commercials that make having your period look hip and fashionable? As though tampon brand selection will not only make you feel prettier, it will make for a better period experience. I have yet to enjoy my period...maybe I'm choosing the wrong brand? Likely not. Period-product branding seems to be so cheesy and full of unbecoming examples of why the merchandise works better (blue liquid, crotch shots during sports, etc.) That makes you wonder who's writing these ads. The everyday woman of today knows what the product does; it seems that the commercials are perhaps giving a play by play to help men or children understand what happens. Let's take this product out of the old-fashioned, disturbing, "how-it-functions" diagrams (as means of advertising) to find some more creative, dynamic mediums. That brings me to the writing style of my book. This book is written for the modern woman. What do I mean by modern? I mean the woman who wants to learn new strategies, dynamic thinking, is confident to take the first steps, feels good about her, and knows she is fabulous.

News flash: Residential home purchases and sales is a female saturated industry.

According to the National Association of REALTORS'®' 2012 *Profile of Home Buyers and Sellers*, "Single FABULOUS women make up eighteen percent of home-owners — compared to ten percent of single men." The report notes that single women have been buying homes at almost twice the rate of single men since the mid-1990s.

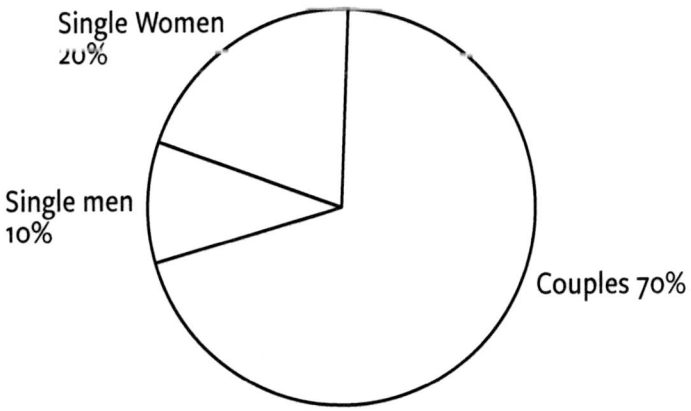

not intended to solicit those under contract

http://www.realtor.org/field-guides/field-guide-to-women-homebuyers

In 2013, this ratio changed to over twenty percent of homeowners being single women. Why have we not done more to gear THIS domestic product (reflecting back on my tampon ad analogy) towards a more comprehensive and rewarding experience for women?

Being a Greater Toronto Area REALTOR®, I myself have bought and sold many homes, including some of my own. I was faced with many challenges as much of the communication in the industry comes from the male voice. Not that there is anything wrong with this. I am not attempting to correct anything, I am merely hoping to enhance the real estate information we, as REALTORS®, provide. As a woman, I want to make an alternative available to our female demographic specifically. I want this Canadian based guide to ENSURE the information will be comprehensive, "woman-centric," and interesting. None of the information is dumbed down or condescending. It is simply and wittingly written through the voice of an honest and good intentioned girlfriend, (which is me). I spare you the shop talk, self-glory, and hidden propaganda. This is not a *"Christine Denty's Get Rich Quick with Real Estate"* guide. The more you are able to understand this business of buying and selling homes, the more rewarding it will be for you. This is your invaluable real estate manual written FOR women, BY a woman .

You Will Survive This, Maybe

I waited to write this chapter until I was going through a particular transition myself. This is one of the primary reasons I wrote this book. It isn't just for the sake of being a woman. This is for the sake of changing your inner dialogue, inner spirit, and outlook as a woman managing a move. I want to help you get through this important event in your life.

I just left my second husband (yes, I know, how terrible), and two months ago, I moved into a townhouse. My stomach is still in knots. I feel completely insecure and I am hyper-sensitive to...EVERYTHING! I feel like some of my friends who should have stepped up to the plate haven't, and others have, whom I didn't expect to do so. Someone I thought was my best friend has made me question the mere existence of a best friend. That label, best friend, is now a painful over-statement. My whole world is upside down. The stress level has brought down my immune system. Everything is out of whack...my period is out of whack! I have been menstrual flow-free for only three out of the eight weeks since I moved! What the hell! Menopause now??? WHY NOW????

I have had a set of new rolling racks that need to be assembled, still in their boxes and sitting in my foyer, for five weeks. My ex got them for me as a peace gesture. How lovely. They have now become part of the décor. I put my keys on them and hang my purse on them. They have become the symbol of my insecurity and lack of turning the page to adjusting to a new life on my own. I have not adjusted, therefore these stupid, rolling-rack boxes remain. They are the objects that keep me captive in my inner prison. One day I might unpack the other three-quarters of my clothes and hang them on these racks so I can start living a normal life again. Maybe.

I'm tearing up right now as I type these words. I am hanging onto hope that I will come through for myself, my kids, and my job. Can I count on me? Maybe.

My driveway is a joke. I haven't been able to chip away at the snow there, which is now a mountain of hard ice. There is no one else responsible for this but me. God, please make it melt! Something make it melt! My neighbours probably hate me. They think I am "that" neighbour who won't mow her lawn or clean up the garbage on it.

My friends and family probably think I'm stupid for leaving him. They probably wonder why I can't get my shit together. They think I'm a home wrecker for leaving and tearing my family apart. Will I survive this?

*not intended to solicit those under contract

The Girlfriend's Fabulous Guide to Real Estate

    Moving out on your own (with or without kids) is a big deal. It is going to be ok. Not today, not tomorrow...not even next week. But one day you WILL be ok. Even if you don't think it now, take it from me, YOU WILL BE OK. I am knee-deep in boxes and chores, and I know I will be ok. Women for centuries have had to do the same thing. They left their husbands, became widowed, got new jobs, bought new houses for the first time, moved in with a lover, lost their jobs, needed to downsize...

    Good news – my kids didn't starve to death. Laundry got done somehow, the cat is still shitting in JUST the litter box, and the snow mountain finally melted.

    Folks, the snow melted.

    I will be ok. I am going to tackle this one day at a time. One good day this week will turn into two good days next week, and three the week after. Will there be a fourth? Now I'm pushing it. In time I will look back at this event as the past that had to happen to bring me to where I am today. Great things do exist on the other side of fear. After this move, I will realize what a strong person looks like when looking in the mirror. You got this girlfriend.

*not intended to solicit those under contract

Real Estate Truths and Myths

This is the second reason why I wrote this book.

It seems that it would take your neighbour, brother, best friend, or work colleague ONE (maybe two) home-sale experiences to consider him or herself an expert in the field. I am not saying that buying and selling homes is rocket science. 'Cause it's not. When it comes to any decisions involving large sums of money, you should consult with a professional at ALL times. In the real estate market, consulting a REALTOR® is the best course of action. Am I biased? Darn right I am. A REALTOR® lives and breathes real estate. Your neighbour, brother, best friend, and work colleague likely have other, more important, hobbies – yes, hobbies, which they know more about and spend countless hours mastering. Their interest in real estate (unless they dive into it full-time, or have a portfolio of properties they manage) is a hobby. This section addresses some of the truths and myths about real estate that seem to circle around our industry.

1. You save money selling privately.
2. You don't need a home inspector to inspect a home – a contractor will do.
3. Overprice your home so that the buyers feel like they are getting a deal when you offer to accept less for it.
4. Underprice a purchase so the sellers will think their home is worth less.
5. You can knock the price down after a home inspection.
6. REALTORS® all do the same work, so choose the one who is cheaper.
7. Male REALTORS® are more aggressive and will fight for a better price than a female will.
8. The REALTOR® who tells you s/he can sell your home higher than market value (or higher than the other REALTOR'S® assessment of market value) is the one you should choose to sell your home.
9. A REALTOR® who drives a nice car is therefore successful.

not intended to solicit those under contract

10. The selling REALTOR® makes all the commission.
11. Staging doesn't make a difference in the sale of your home, so save your money.
12. You don't have to get rid of all the garbage or debris on the closing, as the buyers will do it afterwards.
13. Once a sale is firm it HAS to close on the closing date or else...
14. All lawyers are created equal.
15. Multiple offers means selling for higher than the listing price.
16. REALTORS® who have been practicing for a hundred years must be better than those who have been doing it for just a year or two. Those with an assistant or a team must be even better.
17. Those professionals involved in the buying and selling process, (home inspectors, lawyers, REALTORS®, mortgage lenders, etc.) have to always be honest. There is no such thing as cheating the system or taking shortcuts, as they are professionals and will not risk losing their jobs to do so.
18. Every house will get insurance.
19. A power of sale is a guarantee to pay less than what the property is worth.

All these truths and myths will be addressed in one way or another in the text of this book. I feel that it's important I do this, in order to act on my responsibility of maintaining integrity in the industry of buying and selling homes.

How to Use This Book

I don't expect that you will read the material in this book in order. It is designed to help you during the phase you are going through NOW. I could have published three separate books to cover the home acquisition and selling cycle, but it didn't make sense to deny my reader the luxury of being able to preview the possible next step in her real estate venture. Fumble around this book as you please, refer some information to your friends, and always consult a professional when necessary, even if you feel confident in the information provided. Policies change, the market changes, and unfortunately, a published book will stay in its original state until it is rewritten. Always consult with a professional when selling your home to ensure you are following up to date regulations and rules.

not intended to solicit those under contract

An Overview of Real Estate in Canada

Venturing into the purchase or sale of a home is a big decision. It is important to know what is affecting the prices of homes, in order to understand why you may be offering a certain amount for a property, or why you are being offered a certain amount. I have rarely had a discussion with a homeowner (or someone who is soon to be) without hearing a reaction to the current prices. Of late it has been about how high the homes have been selling for. My clients ask me if prices will continue to increase, and if they could be taking on market risk by paying too much for a home. We as REALTORS® do not have crystal balls. Similar to investment advisors, we have past-market data that helps us see what trend may be occurring at the time. But at best, it is only a mere unpredictable guesstimate – not fact. A home purchase will almost always incur less risk if the investment is held for a longer period of time, as opposed to flipping it in hopes of a continual increase in market value.

Canada is one of the world's wealthiest nations. As with other developed nations, Canada's service industry employs about three-quarters of its workers. Canada is unusual among developed countries in the importance of our natural resources, with the logging and oil industries being two of its most important. Canada also has a sizable manufacturing sector, with the automobile and aircraft industries being especially important. With a long coast line, Canada has the eighth largest commercial fishing and seafood industry in the world. It is also one of the global leaders of the development, maintenance, and publication of software.

Year after year, the state of the economy in Canada directly influences housing sales and prices. When oil prices go down our economy experiences a slump, and real estate can follow suit. Consumers will always have reasons to buy and sell homes, but prices may experience a slower increase and in rare cases, an actual contraction of prices. According to The Canadian Real Estate Association, in 2014 the average home sale price had increased by 5.7% from the same month the prior year. Calgary was among the top three housing markets in 2014. (Toronto and Vancouver were the other two.) Vancouver led as the most expensive housing market in Canada. In the past year (2015) the country wide average home sale price had increased by 12.48%. Toronto increased by 14.96% from last year and Vancouver a whopping 29.71% from last year! This raises my big question, has our income increased by this amount year after year? I think not. At some point will home ownership be unaffordable in our major Canadian cities?

not intended to solicit those under contract

Buying a Home

*not intended to solicit those under contract

Buyer Timeline*

This chapter will cover everything you need to know as a home buyer. Review the timeline to have an idea as to what steps you need to take and when. Not knowing where you are going will affect the end result. In the purchase of a home you have to know your future steps to make the right decision in the moment.

Timeline:

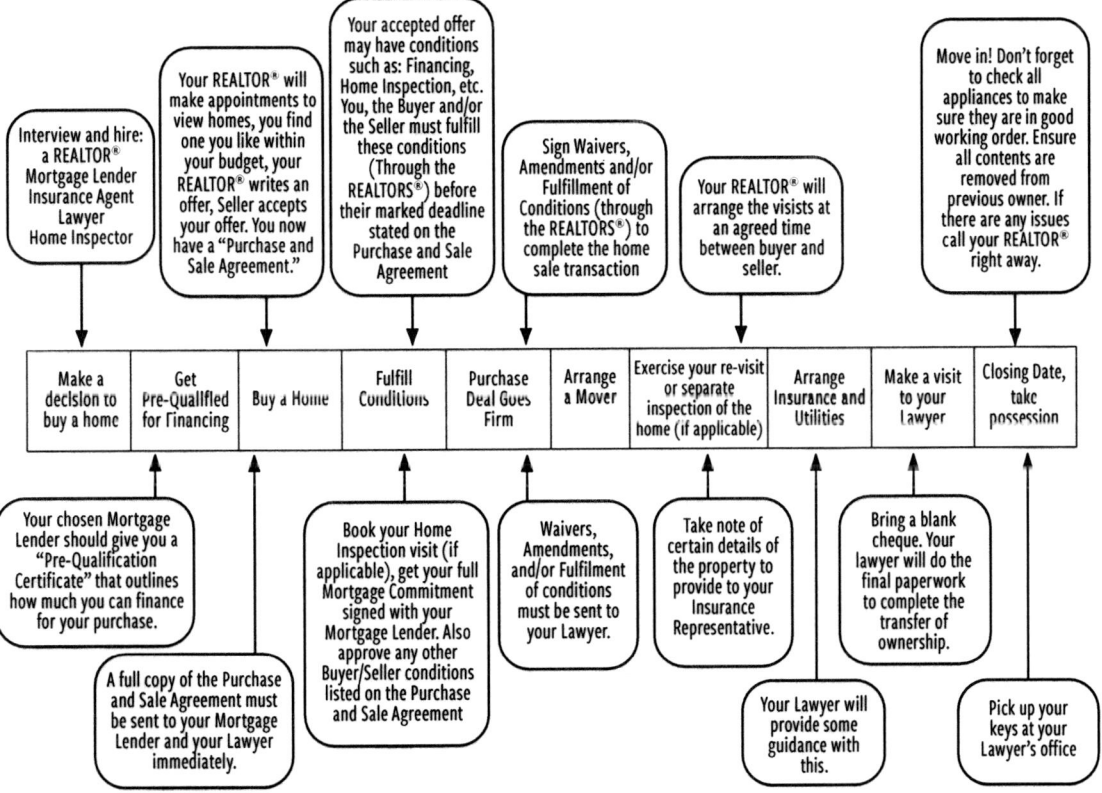

*not intended to solicit those under contract

IMPORTANT CONTACTS:

Professionals Hired:	Phone #'s	Email
REALTOR*:		
Mortgage Lender:		
Lawyer:		
Home Inspector:		
Mover:		

DATES TO REMEMBER:

Detail	Date	Date
Condition fulfillment dates:		
Home inspection date:		
Extra visit dates:		
Lawyer's appointments		
Mortgage Lender appointments:		

*not intended to solicit those under contract

Financing your Purchase

This topic has been addressed first for one very good reason...You MUST get pre-approved for a mortgage before shopping for a home. I cannot stress enough the downside of not knowing your financial position before falling in love with a house. I think the diagram below shows it clearly:

You need to make an appointment with a mortgage lender. (Ask your REALTOR® who s/he recommends, or see a banker with whom you feel comfortable.) Getting pre-approved means that your lender will add up all the numbers, including your down payment, your income, and your monthly obligations to see how much is left over to actually pay for a mortgage, property taxes, utilities, and maybe even condo fees. The more successful you are at fulfilling their requests for information and documentation, the better the outcome you will have. Once you are approved for a mortgage and you are ready to buy, make sure to make funds available for the deposit to an offer (withdraw from RSP or TFSA, mutual funds, etc). You will need to drop off a certified draft to the selling brokerage within 24 hours of having your

*not intended to solicit those under contract

offer accepted. Even if it is a Sunday. It is recommended that you submit $5000-$10,000 to show good faith in your offer of the home you wish to purchase.

Pre-Qualification Certificate

You should ask for a "Pre-Qualification Certificate," if not offered one once your pre-qualification is approved. This shows the lender's commitment to finance a mortgage (for up to ninety days of approval) and assures your REALTOR® that you are ready to shop. Even if you are "Miss Money Bags" and have always had R1 credit rating, you are never too good to carry around one of these certificates. When fighting it out in multiple offers for the house you can't live without, this piece of paper can come in very handy, especially when your competing buyers DON'T have one. Ask your lender to show you exactly what your mortgage payments will look like, as in how much and for how long. Use the worksheet in the "Carrying Costs" on pages 21 to visualize your financial outlay.

ABC Financial
1 Bay St
Toronto, Ontario
M1M 1M1

01/01/2016

Dear Sirs:

Re: Mortgage Loan Pre-Approval
Loan # 12345678

Name:	Role:
Jenn Doe	Principle Applicant

ABC Financial Ltd ("ABC Financial") is pleased to advise that on the basis of information provided in connection with your request for financing, your application for a mortgage loan ("the Loan") has been pre-approved subject to the following terms and conditions. Note this is not a commitment to lend.

Loan Amount	$342,973.75	Rate Guarantee Start	01/01/2016
Current Interest Rate*	3.24%	Rate Guarantee End	04/30/2016
Term (months)	60	Term Type	Closed
Amortization (months)	300	Rate Type	Fixed
Payment Amount	$1,665.64	Payment Frequency	Monthly
Insurance Premium	$10,473.75		

*ABC Financial includes a 0.20% (20 basis points) premium on all pre-approved interest rates. When you find your home, your final CMLS rate will be the lesser of the prevailing interest rate on your pre-approved rate at the date your pre-approval becomes a real application.

Pre-Approval is subject to the following conditions:

1. Stated income does not qualify. If stated income was used to qualify for this pre-approval, this certificate is not redeemable and a new full application should be submitted.
2. Approval by the insurer when your pre-approval becomes a real application.
3. A property evaluation that is acceptable to ABC Financial.
4. This pre-approval document supersedes any previously issued documents relating to this loan.
5. A full credit review at the time of your pre-approval becomes a real application.
6. Condominium ("Condos") are not acceptable. If the property you choose is a Condo, this pre-approval is not redeemable, and a new full application must be subitted.

What if You Have Bad Credit?

Financing can be much more difficult to acquire if you have bad credit. You should know off-hand if you are making all your credit payments on time and whether you carry high balances, etc. A credit score is how a lender rates your credit-worthiness. Usually the score will fall between 500-900, with 500 being the worst and 900 nothing short of going straight to Credit Heaven. The bank, if you are approved, may charge you a higher rate of interest for your mortgage and/or require a higher down payment if your credit score isn't good. If you are planning your purchase in advance, and you are not sure where you stand, do order a copy of your credit report from Equifax (www.equifax.ca) and from Trans Union (www.transunion.ca). This is a good measure to take in advance, so that you can correct anything that could cost you big bucks in trying to secure financing for your future home.

What is CMHC?

Lenders require mortgage loan insurance for loans made to anyone who wishes to purchase a home under $1,000,000 with less than 20% of the purchase price. The Canadian Bank Act prohibits most federally-regulated lending institutions from providing mortgages without mortgage loan insurance for amounts that exceed 80% of the value of the home, or for purchases with less than 20% down payment.

Through your lender, CMHC (Canadian Mortgage and Housing Corporation) Mortgage Loan Insurance enables you to finance up to 95% of the purchase price of a home. Loan to Value refers to the percentage of the purchase price of the home you are financing. The premium is charged on your mortgage amount.

You will typically need to have a minimum down payment starting at 5%. For a purchase price of $500,000 or less, the minimum down payment is 5%. When the purchase price is above $500,000, the minimum down payment is 5% for the first $500,000 and 10% for the remaining portion per CMHC new 2016 guidelines.

Therefore if you are financing 65% of the purchase of a $400,000 home, your mortgage would be $260,000, and the premium of 0.60% equaling $1560 would be split into twelve payments and added right onto the mortgage at the time of financing. (Taxes are extra and charged separately.)

Conversely if you are putting down only the minimum of 5% of the purchase price, your premium would be $11,970 per year, split into twelve payments or paid up front.

Loan-to-Value Ratio	Standard Premium (Effective May 1st, 2014)
Up to and including 65%	0.60%
Up to and including 75%	0.75%
Up to and including 80%	1.25%
Up to and including 85%	1.80%
Up to and including 90%	2.40%
Up to and including 95%	3.15%
90.01% to 95% Non-Traditional Down Payment	3.35%

What do GDS and TDS Mean?

Gross Debt Service

The GDS ratio looks at your new monthly housing costs (mortgage payments, taxes, heating costs, and 50% of condominium fees, if applicable) in relation to your income (before taxes). This amount should be no more than 32% of your gross monthly income.

	EXAMPLE	YOUR CALCULATION
Mortgage Payment (Including Interest)	Mortgage Payment $1000	Proposed Mortgage Payment _____
+	+	+
Property Taxes	Property Taxes $250	Property Taxes (annual amount / 12) _____
+	+	+
Heat / Hydro	Heat / Hydro $150	Heat / Hydro (if unknown put in $150) _____
_____ divided by _____	_____ divided by _____	_____ divided by _____
Gross Monthly Income	Gross Monthly Income $4400	Your Gross Monthly Income _____
X 100	X 100	X 100
= GDS	= 31.81% (GDS)	= _____ % (GDS)

Total Debt Service

The TDS ratio looks at your total monthly debt obligations (including housing costs, loans, lines of credit, car payments, and credit card bills) in relation to your income. Your TDS ratio should be no more than 40% of your gross monthly income.

	EXAMPLE	YOUR CALCULATION
Mortgage Payment (Including Interest)	Mortgage Payment $1000	Proposed Mortgage Payment _____
+	+	+
Property Taxes	Property Taxes $250	Property Taxes (annual amount / 12) _____
+	+	+
Heat / Hydro	Heat / Hydro $150	Heat / Hydro (if unknown put in $150) _____
+	+	+
Other debts: (personal loans, car loans, credit cards, etc.) minimum monthly payment	Other debts: (personal loans, car loans, credit cards, etc.) minimum monthly payments $400	Other debts: (personal loans, car loans, credit cards, etc.) minimum monthly payments _____
_____ divided by _____	_____ divided by _____	_____ divided by _____
Gross Monthly Income	Gross Monthly Income $4400	Your Gross Monthly Income _____
x 100	x 100	x 100
= TDS	= 40.90% (TDS)	= _____% (TDS)

not intended to solicit those under contract

Including Financing as a Condition of the Purchase of a Home

If you need to borrow funds to purchase a home, when should your REALTOR® waive financing as a condition on a sale?
RARELY EVER.

There is a very good reason for this. Up until lately, financing a home has been pretty straightforward. But recent lending policies have become more strict. You may pass the lending test with flying colours and acquire a pre-qualification certificate, but that doesn't mean the bank or CMHC (if applicable) wants to lend on the actual house you are buying. For this reason alone, caution must be taken when waiving your financing.

Once you have a sale that is conditional on financing, you need to contact your lender as soon as possible. They will require some property details, the Purchase and Sale Agreement, and a copy of the MLS listing. They will order a bank appraisal, which will take place within days of the sale. You will need to provide your buying REALTOR'S® contact info, so that s/he can provide the selling REALTOR'S® contact info, and an appointment can be made with the sellers to allow for the appraisal to take place in their home. (See why you have to contact your lender right away???)

The appraiser will determine the bank's opinion on the market value of the home and how much you should be paying for it. A variance of a few thousand is not a big deal. But there are times when the appraiser may want to give the buyer's head a shake and deem the property worth much less. If the appraisal comes up short of the sale price, you may have to cough up more money to bridge the gap between what you were *going* to pay for it and what the bank thinks you *should* pay for it. If you have truckloads of money sitting around to pay the extra funds required to save the deal, then go ahead and waive financing. If you do not, then I advise you leave the financing condition in the sale until the bank has done its due diligence and guarantees you the mortgage.

Your home inspection or fulfillment of other conditions that could require costs should be scheduled for a date after you know you will be approved for your financing. Otherwise you have spent $400 for an inspection on a home you can't buy.

Housing Options

For the purpose of simplicity, I will only discuss the two most common housing options: Resale Houses and Condos (condo towns, condo apartments).

Houses

With a house, you are the owner of the building and the land it sits on. This is called "fee simple" ownership. This means you own the piece of land, the structure on it, and the air above it. You control the amount of heat you use, the water you run, and the electricity you power up. Any costs associated with repair and maintenance are typically your own (unless you rent appliances and/or the hot water tank). Apart from requiring a permit, you can make structural and aesthetic changes as desired. This can substantially increase (or in some cases decrease) the value of the home. Location in a major urban district, or conversely, an elite rural area, can affect the price even more than the features of the house itself. We've all heard the saying, "Location, location, location." There is no exception to this when it comes to real estate.

When you're buying a resale home, your REALTOR® will usually recommend that you get a home inspection. This may or may not be deemed mandatory in the conditions of a written offer, but nevertheless, it is always a good idea to have one when you are seriously considering the purchase of a particular home. If you are going to have a home inspection done, you may as well include it as a condition of sale. Reason being, if there is a major structural issue, you could be entitled to knock off some of the price you offered or even to break off the sale if the issue is serious enough. A good home inspector will examine the exterior of the house, the roof, driveway, structural integrity, safety, electrical, water and heat systems, ventilation, the presence of moisture, and lots more. A thorough inspection takes about three hours, and you and your REALTOR® must be present during it.

Owning a home can be very rewarding, but you must follow a home maintenance plan to keep its value, aesthetics, and system functionality in top-notch shape. You can attempt to manage these activities yourself or you can hire a professional. In further graphs I have included a cost of $200/month for exterior maintenance. You do save money doing it yourself, but take into account the level of difficulty and the safety of the task. There is nothing wrong with hiring a professional to do it – what counts is that it is getting done.

Condos

With a condominium, you only get the exclusive right to the interior space of your dwelling unit, but the land, walls, grounds, fences, and facilities are owned in common with the other owners in the complex. Considered part of the common elements are: windows, electrical, plumbing, and heating. Common forms of condominiums are: condo-townhouses, apartments, co-operative apartment buildings, and resort properties. A condo can offer a lifestyle that is quite appealing to those who want an "all-in" living experience. Many are located by a scenic body of water, city centre, and/or other kinds of attractions.

When you're buying a resale condo, your REALTOR® will put some conditions in for your protection. One in particular is the inclusion (within ten days of the acceptance of an offer) of a "Status Certificate." This is ordered by the selling agent and the cost of about $100-$150 is usually transferred to the seller. The status certificate, funnily enough, has nothing to do with certificates and determining a "status" on the property is not black and white. It is a lengthy document detailing:

- All the uses of the property.
- What is covered in damage.
- Financial status of a unit and of the condo corporation.
- What the fees are.
- Any large increase of maintenance fees that is going to come into effect.
- Any special assessment that is being contemplated by the board.
- Any arrears or liens that a particular suite might have.

In addition, it contains the condo declaration, by-laws, budget, reserve fund, insurance, management contract, rules, minutes of the last annual general meeting, and mention of any lawsuit involving the corporation. This document can run into one hundred barely legible pages. Your real estate lawyer will call you in to review it to ensure the condo is run properly, and there are no surprises or indications of a substantial rise in fees. Typically, this potential action is written in the conditions, and you can decide to move forward or to decline the purchase, based on your lawyer's opinion of the Status Certificate details. No condo purchase can have the condition of lawyer's review of this certificate waived.

Any costs for repairs or upgrades of the structure or mechanical systems of the condo should be covered by the condo corporation. But interior renos of the suite, which include changing the plumbing or electrical, are expected to be at your cost (e.g.: kitchen or bathroom reno) and must be approved by the condo board prior to demolition.

Your REALTOR® may recommend a condo inspection. This inspection is similar to a regular home inspection, except any deficiencies regarding the exterior of the home, which the condo corporation is in charge of, are forwarded to the condo corporation for the property manager to remedy: windows, fire door, roof, brick, tree roots, foundation, walkways, driveways, structural safety, exterior electrical panels, etc. This can get very tricky as property managers are not directly affected by the sale, and therefore can drag their feet at times, or may even dispute the work that needs to get done. In my experience, though, I've dealt with mostly good and only a few bad property managers.

Your REALTOR® needs to contact the condo corporation if there are any issues with remedial work to be done. How the work is being handled may be a deciding factor for you in whether or not you want to move forward with the purchase.

Issues right at sale may echo through your many years of condo ownership. If all is handled well, this is a good indication that you would be a satisfied condo owner moving forward.

Buyer's Closing Costs

So now you are searching for the home of your dreams? Sorry to burst your bubble, but it's time to discuss the crappy part. Closing costs are a reality to buying a home. Typically, we recommend that you reserve 1.5% for closing costs. For example, on a $400,000 purchase, you should set aside $6000 for these costs. Listed are the common costs to buying a home.

Land Transfer Tax

Tax, tax, tax...inevitable. Real estate is no exception. I'm not sure where the term "Land Transfer" comes from, as we can't pick up the piece of land and carry it to another location. But nevertheless...here it is...the dreadful Land Transfer Tax. More information can be found at:

> http://www.fin.gov.on.ca/en/tax/ltt/

Tax Rates

The tax rates calculated on the value of the consideration are:

- 0.5% up to and including $55,000
- 1% above $55,000 up to and including $250,000
- 1.5% above $250,000
- 2% above $400,000 when the land contains one or two single-family residences.

The land transfer tax rate is the same for residents and non-residents of Canada. These are always subject to change.

Calculating the Tax Amount

Use the table below to calculate land transfer tax on a residential home purchase.

- Residential property: land that contains one or two single family residences
- PP: Purchase Price
- LTT: Land transfer tax payable

Purchase Price:	LTT = Land Transfer Tax PP= Purchase Price Formula:
Up to and including $55,000	LTT = PP x 0.005
above $55,000 and up to $250,000	LTT = (PP x 0.01) - $275
above $250,000 and up to $400,000	LTT = (PP x 0.015) - $1525
above $400,000	LTT = (PP x 0.02) - $3525

To calculate the land transfer tax on a $450,000 purchase:

($350,000 x 0.015) - $1525

$5250-$1525 = $3725

Land Transfer Tax = $3725

Legal Fees

Lawyers vary in pricing; $400-$800, not including disbursements. It is not a bad thing to take your REALTOR®'s opinion on whom to use if you don't have a lawyer in mind. A busy REALTOR® works with lawyers quite a bit. Also, if you have a friend, co-worker, or family member who has had a good experience with someone, this is also a good place to start. It's a good idea to look them up at the Better Business Bureau, as well to see if there have been any real issues in the past. http://www.bbb.org/

Mortgage Insurance

As discussed earlier, this is a separate payment paid to the insurer of your mortgage, commonly the Canadian Mortgage and Housing Corporation. CMHC is a federally-owned entity dedicated to regulation and the insurance of high-ratio mortgages. If you are putting less than 20% as a down payment, the lender requires that your mortgage be insured for risk to yourself, the seller, and the lender. The premium is typically added to your new mortgage balance, but the HST on the premium is owed separately.

Title Insurance

Title Insurance is sometimes included in your mortgage through your lender. It protects your ownership or title against losses incurred as a result of undetected or unknown title defects, for as long as you own your home. Even if you are the rightful owner of a home, there are instances such as real estate fraud, when your title can come into question. Title insurance continues to protect your ownership from the day of closing, to the day you sell your home. The fee is typically $250-$300.

Property Tax and Utility Adjustments

When you visit your lawyer's office to sign all closing documentation, you will likely be required to bring in a certified cheque or bank draft representing all adjustments to the purchase price. Adjustments may include items that have been prepaid beyond the closing date by the seller and benefit the purchaser beyond the closing date. A credit will be given to the seller as an adjustment on closing. For example, if your closing date is May 21st, the seller has likely already prepaid the property taxes until May 31st. The purchaser is responsible for all property expenditures from May 21st onward, and therefore the seller is to receive a credit for the overpaid taxes from May 21st to May 31st.

Property Appraisal

Your lender may have had to order a property appraisal to make sure you did not pay too much for the house they are financing for you. Not all lenders charge for this separately. But some do. This ranges between $150-$200.

Mortgage Application Fee

Your lending institution may charge a fee for processing your mortgage application. These costs vary. If you are testing the water for an approval you will definitely be charged as the lender deserves to be paid for their time. If the lender knows you are situationally motivated to borrow you can usually get this fee waived as you will be following through with your venture.

Home Inspection

If you have opted to have a home inspection done, the fee will be required either at the time of the inspection booking, or right after the inspection. It can range between $300-$500 for a standard inspection, but can go up depending on how many families the home can house (multi-family, duplex, triplex, etc.) and other irregular factors.

Interest Adjustment

Interest adjustment (IAD – interest adjustment date on the mortgage commitment document) is calculated from the proposed date of advancement of the loan, to your projected first payment date. On your first payment, technically your interest is past due and you must catch up. Because the mortgage payment system does not allow for charging you this amount with the first payment, the interest is therefore due upon advancement of your mortgage. Lawyers routinely collect interest adjustments at closing.

Carrying Costs

Home Ownership Carrying Cost

Carrying costs for a home are determined by your usage, and they can be greatly controlled based on your lifestyle and particular needs. When you are applying for a mortgage, the carrying costs considered are the mortgage payment, property tax, and utilities. Let's get to reality now. There are more out-of-pocket expenses. The true common ownership costs are:

- mortgage
- property tax
- utilities (heat/hydro/water)
- exterior maintenance
- home insurance

This is not to say these are your only costs. But they are typical and should be expected.

Condo Carrying Cost

Condo fees can vary and are a big consideration when applying for a mortgage and weighing out your monthly ownership costs. The fees will typically (but not always) include building insurance, a parking space, building and property maintenance, use of facilities (gym, entertainment room, pool), and sometimes heat/hydro/water. Typically your ownership costs per month would be:

- mortgage
- property tax
- condo fees

- heat/hydro/water (if not included in the condo fees)
- home insurance (not typical but sometimes recommended. Consult with a home insurance agent)

Comparison between a House and Condo

In the example below, you can see that expenses are all relative, even though they are paid differently for a house or a condo. Every home requires payments for a mortgage, taxes, heat/water/electricity, and insurance. No two properties will have equal costs for any of the items listed, but this example poses the idea of noting these costs in comparison to each other.

Assumption: all have a mortgage payment of $850 and property taxes of $250 per month

Monthly Costs:	Condo 1	Condo 2	Condo 3	House 1
Mortgage Payment	$850	$850	$850	$850
Property Taxes	$225	$225	$225	$225
Utilities	$0	$150	$0	$200
Property Maintenance	$0	$0	$0	$200
Home Insurance	N/A	N/A	N/A	$75
Maintenance Fee	$300	$300	$500	N/A
Carrying Cost	**$1375**	**$1525**	**$1575**	**$1550**

Having an equal mortgage payment and property taxes for different properties does not indicate that your costs will be the same between houses, or between different condos. One must take in all the factors involved, even between one condo and another. Sometimes condo fees are higher because buildings are getting older and require repair...they are *not* indicative of a better building. A "property maintenance" cost was added to the house to consider the cost of exterior maintenance (mowing the lawn, shoveling, pruning, gutter cleaning, etc.) This has been included because homeowners would either have to pay for the service anyway or use their own valuable time to do the work. Time is money. With condos, these services are being done for you and are paid for by your condo fees.

Use this worksheet to calculate the costs associated with the home of your dreams (or at least the one you are considering). Not all of these numbers are discussed by your banker when you apply for financing, but you must know them for yourself. Home ownership comes with lots of hidden costs; you should at least be familiar with some of the typical expenditures you will be getting yourself into.

Basic Carrying Cost Worksheet

Worksheet - Basic Carrying Costs:
Address:_____

Monthly Costs: | Your Potential Monthly Costs:

- Mortgage
- Property Taxes
- Utilities: heat, hydro, water
- Property Maintenance
- Home Insurance
- Condo Fees (if applicable)
- Other (security system, pool maintenance, etc.)

Monthly Total:

not intended to solicit those under contract

Home Inspection

Imagine this...

A person puts on a tacky tool belt and meets you at your "soon to be" home. He then pulls, pokes, cranks, turns on, smells, crawls into, shimmies up, hovers over, and points lights into every nook and cranny, to detect any mini or large nightmares you might encounter while owning that home. That turbo-nerd also has gadgets that would cause you to second guess your future conduct in that same home for the fear of the NEXT turbo nerd discovering your dirty little secrets. But waiving the option to have "Inspector Gadget" find minor and major issues is not recommended. Would you marry someone you just met? Hmmm, didn't think so.

Hiring a certified home inspector is essential to ensuring that the home inspection is conducted to a recognized standard, providing you with valuable information about the condition of the home. The certification process is foggy at best, but the more credentials your home inspector has, the more educated you will be in deciding on the purchase of your home. At the inspector's discretion, a list of minor building flaws or small repairs and maintenance items may be provided, as a courtesy.

Thermal Imaging:

This may very well be one of the most indispensable value- added home inspection services offered. This service has many valuable uses:... if you suspect you have a leak.. If, you have a visual leak but cannot identify it's source., (Why tear down walls before we have a look?) If you suspect that there is major air infiltration that is affecting the energy costs of your home. If you see signs of previous moisture. The possibilities are endless.

Using thermal imaging in home inspections will:

- Extend the inspector's ability to inspect the house.
- Help find conditions that would otherwise go unnoticed.
- Serve as an additional method of verifying defects suspected or found by other means, thus better proving the existence of the defect.

not intended to solicit those under contract

- Provide better understanding of other problems with the house, and their causes.

This is relatively new technology and it can greatly reduce the home buyer's risk of water infiltration, which cannot be seen or detected in a typical home inspection.

Condominium/Townhouse Inspections:

Just like any other major purchase item, condominiums and townhouses should also be inspected before you buy. A thorough inspection of the condominium or townhouse interior examines the structure, mechanics, plumbing, and the electrical and heating/AC systems within the unit, along with any built-in appliances. This inspection takes one to two hours to complete, and it will provide you with all the same information as an extensive home inspection.

Prelisting Home Inspection:

If you're selling, eventually your buyers are going to order a home inspection. You may as well know what they are going to find by getting there first. Having a home inspection performed ahead of time can also help in many other ways:

1. The seller can choose a certified home inspector, rather than be at the mercy of the buyer's choice of home inspector.
2. The seller can schedule the home inspection at the seller's convenience.
3. The inspection might alert the seller of any items of immediate personal concern, such as radon gas or active termite infestation.
4. The seller can assist the home inspector during the inspection, something normally not done during a buyer's home inspection.
5. The seller can have the home inspector correct any misstatements in the home inspection report before it is generated.
6. The report can help the seller realistically price the home if problems exist.
7. The home inspection report can help the seller justify a higher asking price if problems don't exist, or have been corrected.
8. A seller home inspection reveals problems ahead of time, which:
    1. might make the home show better.
    2. gives the seller time to make repairs and shop for competitive contractors.
    3. permits the seller to attach repair estimates or paid invoices to the home inspection report.

8. removes over-inflated buyer-procured estimates from the negotiation table.
9. The home inspection report might alert the seller to any immediate safety issues, before agents and visitors tour the home.
10. The home inspection report provides a third-party, unbiased opinion to offer to potential buyers.
11. A seller-home inspection permits a clean home inspection report to be used as a marketing tool.
12. A seller-home inspection is the ultimate gesture in forthrightness on the part of the seller.
13. The home inspector's report might relieve prospective buyers' unfounded suspicions, before they walk away.
14. A seller-home inspection lightens negotiations and eleventh-hour re-negotiations.
15. The home inspector's report might encourage the buyer to waive the inspection contingency.
16. The deal is less likely to fall apart the way it often does when a buyer's home inspection unexpectedly reveals a problem, last minute.
17. The home inspector's report provides full-disclosure protection from future legal claims.

Copies of the home inspection report, along with receipts for any repairs, should be made available to potential buyers.

Review the home inspection report in the appendix, to see the kinds of issues that can arise during an inspection. Despite all the "red," this home passed the inspection. No home is likely to come up as perfect, because there are issues that just naturally occur behind where we can see them.

APPENDIX AT BACK OF BOOK

Insurance

I should not have to school you on the need for insurance. If I do, put the book down, have a little reality chat with yourself...and when the bulb turns on in your head, pick up this book again.

One of the biggest mistakes a buyer will make is to wait until the last minute to secure an insurance policy. Typically, at the lawyer's desk a few days before closing, the question will arise, "Did you get insurance?" This may be a huge problem. Why? Your mortgage advancement is dependent on you acquiring insurance for the home you are purchasing. Your mortgage representative likely won't urge that you get insurance, nor recommend an insurance agent. There are regulations in place to discourage financial representatives in making recommendations. We won't get into detail about this, but know that this is the case. You may have no one prompting you to get insurance during the process of your home purchase. Why is this risky? No insurance = no mortgage = no sale. To have this outcome is catastrophic, and it could even result in a lawsuit against you for not being able to close the sale on time, if at all, and you could lose your purchase deposit, in order to pay for legal costs.

How do you avoid such an outcome? Secure an insurance agent once you have an offer accepted. As a REALTOR®, for the buyer's protection, I will typically input a condition on the Purchase and Sale Agreement, stating that the sale is contingent on the buyer being able to obtain insurance (more commonly included as a condition for older homes due to wiring and outdated building code issues). This eliminates the risk of the buyer being sued if s/he cannot secure insurance:

"This offer is conditional on the Buyer arranging insurance for the property satisfactory to the Buyer in the Buyer's sole and absolute discretion. Unless the Buyer gives notice in writing delivered to the Seller personally, or in accordance with any other provisions for the delivery of notice in this Agreement of Purchase and Sale or any Schedule thereto not later than 6:00 p.m. on November 14, 2014, that this condition is fulfilled, this offer shall be null and void and the deposit shall be returned to the Buyer in full without deduction. The Seller agrees to co-operate in providing access to the property, if necessary, for any inspection of the property required for the fulfillment of this condition. This condition is included for the benefit of the Buyer and may be waived at the Buyer's sole option by notice in writing to the Seller as aforesaid within the time period stated herein."

If a buyer cannot insure the home s/he is purchasing, the seller may need to re-evaluate its condition and make necessary improvements to ensure a successful future sale and a happy buyer. Just because the home currently has insurance does not necessarily indicate that the home will be insurable in the future.

Adjudication

Being approved for insurance is a lot like getting a mortgage. There is no guarantee that you will be able to get insurance on your new home. It is not very often one gets declined, but it is important to know that it is not a slam-dunk or a no-brainer. Not only does the insurance company need to determine their financial outlay if your home burns to the ground, but they also need to know how likely you are to make frequent or false claims. The number of people living in the home, the home's permitted and/or intended uses, and your living habits are of importance as well. If you have had a home inspection done during the purchase of the property, it is likely the insurance broker will want to see it, to answer questions about the home that you may not know the answer to. Beware that this may complicate the quote, as any defects outlined may need to be addressed immediately, in order for insurance to take place. A red-spotted home inspection may be great for a price reduction when buying the home, but it could bite you in the behind when you are trying to secure insurance.

See the Property Insurance Data Form below and over. This is the typical information an insurance broker will require when deciding whether to sell a policy to you. You can see why this process should not be done at the last minute, as it is quite detailed. When you have an accepted offer on your dream home, give this worksheet to your chosen insurance agent. He or she will love you for it!

HOME INSURANCE DATA FORM - EXTERIOR

STREET ADDRESS:	MORTGAGE AMOUNT:	POSSESSION DATE:	PURCHASE AMOUNT:
	LOAN TO VALUE:	LAWYER'S NAME:	
ARCHITECTURE	YEAR HOME BUILT	MAJOR RENO'S, STRUCTURAL, ADDITIONS, REPAIRS	OTHER INFO
2 STOREY ☐			
3 STOREY ☐			
BUNGALOW ☐			
SPLIT LEVEL ☐			
CONDO APARTMENT ☐			
EXTERIOR	AGE AND TYPE OF ROOF	IMPROVEMENTS OR REPAIRS TO EXTERIOR	OTHER INFO
BRICK ☐			
VINYL ☐			
STUCCO ☐			
WOOD SIDING ☐			
OTHER ☐			
STRUCTURES	YEAR STRUCTURES BUILT	RECENT IMPROVEMENTS TO STRUCTURES	OTHER INFO
GARAGE ☐			
DECK ☐			
POOL ☐			
HOT TUB ☐			
GAZEBO ☐			

HOME INSURANCE DATA FORM - INTERIOR

FLOORING	FLOORING TYPE	YEAR LAID	OTHER INFO
MAIN LEVEL			
UPPER LEVEL			
BASEMENT			
OTHER			
OTHER			
HVAC	AGE OF FURNACE	REPAIRS TO FURNACE (IF KNOWN)	OTHER INFO
AIR CONDITIONING ○yes ○no			
HOT WATER TANK	AGE OF HOT WATER	RECENT REPAIRS TO HOT WATER TANK (IF KNOWN)	OTHER INFO
SIZE			
ELECTRICAL	AGE OF WIRING	RECENT REPAIRS OR IMPROVEMENTS (IF KNOWN)	OTHER INFO
ALUMINUM ☐			
COPPER ☐			
KNOB AND TUBE ☐			

Save Your Policy Information

Put your insurance binder in a safe place. Know what is covered and what is not. Understand the policy's interpretation of "Act of God" and accidental damage. Do not assume that every instance of a flood is covered. There are specific guidelines for replacement, and you need to know if they apply to your situation. The cost of insurance is dependent on what it would cost to replace the house and which additional endorsements or riders are attached to the policy. Most insurers charge a lower premium if it appears less likely the home will be damaged or destroyed. There are specific guidelines for replacement and you need to know if they apply to your situation.

Home buying Scenarios

So you are Leaving your Spouse...

First of all, sorry for what you are going through. Been there, done that, and wrote the book. (Literally!)

Separation and divorce are common realities in today's society. I myself have gone through many cohabitation separations and 2 unpleasant yet quiet divorces. My first divorce was not volatile as I pretty much gave up most of my rights as a mother and wife, and walked away with what seemed fair (at first). But later I realized I was entitled to much more. Had I fought for what I had a right to, it would have been WWIII, and I wasn't up for it. Unfortunately, the papers had been signed under duress, to escape the temporary, one-bedroom basement apartment I was shoved into with my two kids, while leaving him...I struggled financially for many years because of it. Yes I'm still bitter, but at the very least he is a decent father and has a good sense of humour when dealing with girlie-tween issues. I have realized over the years that the kids family unity is more important than money.

There are many questions and not very many straight answers about how to handle the primary residence during a separation. Situations can be volatile at best. Neither partner walks away completely happy or unscarred, and neither do the children. They say a spouse's true colours come out through a divorce. That is a wee bit of a crock of a statement. Separating is one of the most stressful things a person can go through. When under stress and pressure, we tend not to think like our cheery selves. We also get terrible advice from others that don't always apply to our own situations. The worst advice I was given was, "You can revisit the separation agreement afterwards." Yeah right. If I had $20,000 in my bank account for legal costs, sure, let's revisit...

So what now? Where do you go? Do you move out? Can you get your spouse to leave? What about the children?

In most cases, one spouse will tell the other s/he wants to separate. Sometimes it is mutual. In either case, the decision on when to leave, and who should do the leaving is almost never agreed upon. Emotions are raw and tempers rise. The knot in your stomach nauseates you. Regardless of how quickly you would like the terrible feeling to end, you cannot rush where one of you is to end up after leaving the primary residence. I myself rushed it, and I ended up in a one-bedroom basement apartment with my two little girls. I was earning $85,000 a year, yet took the first open door out of my relationship into a crappy ghetto pad. My ex gave me a budget of $600 a month to secure a place to live; luckily I was able to bump it up to $800. He called the shots and had full lockdown on our joint funds.

How does one break free of being taken advantage like this to create a neutral situation? Counselling. A good counsellor will recognize the disadvantage and call out you or your spouse's dominant behavior. The conclusion may end up being that you're the one with issues that are impeding a clean break up. Be open to criticism and take the advice that applies to you. Ask the counsellor what is fair. If s/he doesn't have a straight answer, talk about it in the session. Let the counsellor mediate the discussion. Once something is agreed upon, then you and your spouse should commit to that action. If this doesn't work, you may have to take the softer road and enter into a less ideal residence, in exchange for your sanity. If you have children, they should be your first priority. You both brought them into this world, and they deserve security at all times. In the end, I hate to say it, but – "It's just money." No one's life, security, sanity, or health is worth risking, in order to getting further ahead financially during a separation. You're a smart cookie; you can make it back after you are free from a situation full of burdens and grief. I don't believe in Karma, but I do believe in one special kind of revenge. It's called, "Become successful and tune into your inner happiness to make your ex jealous." It usually works well.

I will not discuss creative ways to get more money out of a separation, as this is unethical (and I am sure some of your close friends will fill your head with lots of not so great ideas). Take the high road so you don't have a vengeful ex, who is ready to pull the trigger years down the road because of your potential greed.

A REALTOR® should only come into the picture once the separation agreement is signed and completed. I have been called into play in the middle of a separation and been caught in the line of fire. I got thrown into the volatility and ended up firing my clients, as I became tired of the calls from each spouse complaining about the situation ten times a day. I was merely a glorified pin-cushion with a nice pair of designer shoes. I remember my second sale I ever had; I was yo-yo'd in the husband and wife's emotions and got caught up in it. I cried on the couch for 2 hours because I was afraid of losing the sale and having unhappy clients. Please for all REALTORS® sake do not pull us into the drama. It makes for a volatile sale. We have plenty in our own lives to manage.

Buying a rental property...

This is not for the faint at heart. Delinquent tenants, or worse, "career" tenants can make your investment experience a horrible one that you would like to forget. When choosing a REALTOR® to assist you, make sure that s/he has experience in the purchase and sale of rental properties, as well as having done the deed personally. If conducted correctly, the property investment business can be very lucrative, and it can create a nice nest egg for retirement.

Qualifying Process

Three of the most important factors in choosing a rental property...

1. There is a demand for rentals in the area and a low vacancy rate.
2. The property itself is likely to go up in value.
3. The property itself is likely to go up in value.

Did you see what I did there? The equity-growth factor is commonly missed when qualifying a property, as investors like to see the rental income dollars. Overlooking a property's ability to grow in value over time can cause a huge disappointment when unloading it down the road. Not to mention the extra pressure to reduce vacancy. If you are not earning every dollar each month, you could find yourself in a losing position. Not quite what you were aiming for.

It is best to seek a property in an area that:

- is close to transportation to a major city (i.e.: Toronto, Vancouver, etc.)
- is desirable yet affordable.
- has a low unemployment rate.
- is not saturated with rental properties.
- doesn't have a high amount of listings and vacancies.
- has a low crime rate.

- has reasonable property taxes.
- has amenities close by.

Your ideal tenants should be working class (or pension earners), goal-oriented individuals who are renting because:

- buying a home is their next goal (young couple).
- they desire a more private living space (leaving the nest).
- they don't want the chore of home ownership (seniors).
- they are not home enough to enjoy property ownership.
- they are required to move because of their job.
- they are bridging the gap between a home sale and purchase.

These tenants should have:

- good credit history.
- good rental history.
- no criminal record.
- monthly income that is at least three times the monthly rent.
- no more than one adult per bedroom rented (with the exception of two adults and a baby in one room).
- no smoking rules for themselves and friends.
- ideally no pets – one cat is not too destructive, yet multiple animals and large dogs can be very destructive... be aware of the size and habits of the animal.
- a believable reason as to why they want to pay rent and not buy – if the story doesn't seem to fit, you may have a career tenant at play.

Warning: Some applicants seem like the ideal tenants. Beware; there is a ton of fraud happening in the tenant pool. I've encountered many scenarios, in which the applicant was not the ACTUAL person moving in. Landlords have been mortified to discover that the single mother they thought they were renting to was, in fact, four adult males with the dogs that defecated throughout the home. (True story!) So always put measures in place to make certain that the applicants are the actual people occupying the home.

We won't get into much more detail about rentals, but this brief diagram explains why people go through all the trouble of investing in them...

Initial investment: $40,000
Mortgage: $160,000

Pymt + Ins + Taxes + monthly property maintenance: $1150
Rent charged $1200 + utilities

In the beginning

few years later...
use equity to buy
another rental property

not intended to solicit those under contract

Buying a Property with Someone Else

Buying a property with someone is a big move. (No pun intended.) There are a lot of considerations when getting into the legal contract of owning a home. You may need to have a second person (your love interest, sibling, friend, or parent) help you financially, to buy the home. That person could be asked to be on title (as rightful owner) of the home, per financing provisions. So in simple terms...your mortgage company will make both of you co-owners of the property (joint tenancy), because they need both your incomes to qualify you for the mortgage. Usually, when you buy a house with someone, this is understood and all part of forming a life together. There are other kinds of ownership structures, but the most common for residential properties is *joint tenancy*.

Joint tenancy is an undivided interest in the whole of one property. It creates a right of survivorship. This right provides that if any one of the joint tenants dies, the remainder of the property is transferred to the survivor.

Normally this doesn't pose any problems...But for the purposes of this insightfully specific writing; I will address the most obvious downfall:

If you are not on the same page about selling the house, whether it be due to separation, family issues, job loss, or virtually any disagreement...you may be stuck in home-ownership purgatory until one of you gives in. Sometimes, under duress, rash decisions are made and losses are incurred. A lawyer won't just remove someone off title if both of you are on the mortgage. The finance company won't remove someone off the mortgage unless the remaining borrower qualifies on his or her own to carry it. Even if you are able to carry the mortgage alone, your soon to be ex-partner may refuse to allow it. It's really a game of house-Russian roulette. There is not a lot of advice I can give if both of you can't come to an agreement.

To my next point...do not add someone onto the title of your home (pre-existing ownership) simply for the purpose of showing you care. Yes, you heard me. There are other ways to show you care. You can write your wishes in an up-to-date will, etc. Do not under-estimate the legal bull you will be entwined in, if you add on a partner for illegitimate reasons.

Example: "Tony and Jenn."

Jenn owned a home in Smalltown. She started dating Tony, fell in love, and Tony moved in. Jenn decided to refinance the home and add Tony on title (joint ownership), because he was helping to pay the bills, and she felt it was a good gesture. She also wanted to make sure that if she died, Tony would get to keep the house.

Well, Tony wasn't all he was cracked up to be, and they wanted to break up. Jenn wanted Tony to move out. (But since when does someone move out just because you want him to?) Tony's ultimatum was to sell the house or bust. Jenn just wanted it over so she sold her (well, technically now it was now *their*) home. She lost her initial down payment through real estate fees, and Tony was entitled to half the residual capital left from the sale.

What should Jenn have done? The ideal choice would have been to leave the home to Tony in her will (if appropriate given their relationship). Then, when or if f they broke-up, she could have simply changed the will. Another option would have been to just allow Tony to pay his portion of the mortgage, as it was likely cheaper than rent. Tony could also have made an equal contribution to the existing equity and had a moral right to half at that point. Then Jenn could have gone ahead and added him on title and the mortgage, if he qualified. She should have also had a pre-nup in place to cover her initial investment, in case the relationship ended badly. She would likely have had to hire a lawyer to guarantee that her entitlement per the pre-nup was granted, but in that case she might have been financially further ahead to pay out Tony and call it a day.

We enter into agreements and relationships with innocence and good intentions. Excitement can hardly be contained during the onset of a long-term relationship. It isn't easy to exercise forward planning, in case of a possible break up. But this day and age, with the rate of separations of couples, you owe it to yourself to first protect your investments as much as you can. You can still enjoy a fruitful and loving, long-term union with your financial interests protected. After all, wouldn't your partner want the same for him/herself?

Power of Sales

Ever hear the saying, "You get what you pay for"?

Many of my buyers have the notion that a power of sale is an opportunity to buy a home at a discounted price. Through all of my experience of power of sales, this notion has not rung true. Perhaps explaining with a scenario of how a power of sale comes about might help.

Jenn and Tony have a home with a fairly large mortgage on it from bank ABC. Their finances are not always their first priority, and so their house has become tired because they have not put money into its upkeep. They are happy with the state of their home and don't see the need to invest in repairs until Tony makes more money. But Tony gets laid off from his company and has a hard time finding another job. This puts a financial strain on the couple and they can't meet all their financial obligations on time. Their ABC mortgage is no exception.

Six months go by and there's no job for Tony. He and Jenn can't afford their mortgage payments, and are no longer making them. They try to sell the home before the bank gets serious about their delinquency. Unfortunately because their house has not been kept up very well, there are no buyers interested. One more payment is missed and Tony and Jenn are now over four months behind on their mortgage. The bank gives them forty-five days to remedy the default, otherwise it will take over ownership of their home. The *Mortgage Act* sets out the provisions that allow a home to be sold by the mortgagee as a Power of Sale without judicial proceedings, if default occurs. Tony and Jenn are not able to bring the mortgage to a good standing and are forced to move out.

ABC Bank has an appraisal done to determine the value of the home. This assessed value will likely be the price at which the bank will list the house. When the bank lists the home with a REALTOR® on the MLS, the REALTOR® offers it as a bank power of sale, in 'as is' condition. This means that the bank does NOT guarantee the state or condition of the home – it is truly 'buyer beware.' Therefore, when a buyer enters into this home's purchase contract, it is a final, legally binding contract with no loopholes or ways out. If the toilet falls through the ceiling and there is a toxic amount of mold found in the home, the buyer will be stuck with it. On the flip side, ABC Bank has to make sure there are enough funds from the proceeds of the sale to pay out any property taxes that might be overdue, accumulating interest and legal costs in the whole ordeal. The bank will not sell the property for less than it's worth, in order

not intended to solicit those under contract

to ensure that all *their* obligations are met. They also have a legal obligation to Tony and Jenn to sell it at the highest value possible.

The bank turns off the heat to minimize energy costs and then shuts off the water so that the pipes don't freeze. Usually all appliances are removed, leaving only the bare bones of the home. Details about the age of the roof or any major repairs might be unknown as the bank has just come into ownership recently and the defaulted mortgagor may not be cooperating enough to relay accurate information about the house.

This hardly seems like a deal to me.

There are some cases in which a power of sale could have been imposed due to home owners walking away from a property after deciding they could not manage it, but these instances are very rare. This is not to discourage someone from buying a power of sale property, but it is simply to demonstrate that there is no real deal to be had. You get what you are paying for, and sometimes you actually get less in the end. From one girl to another, unless you have a VERY handy person around and are willing to spend money on lots of surprises, I would caution against a purchase of this kind.

Estate Purchase

Buying an Estate Home

There are some cautionary measures that need to be taken when involved in an estate purchase.

- Confirm property taxes and any liens are paid, up to date, and in good standing.
- Confirm the estate representative is legally allowed to sell the property. (Probate has taken place and estate representatives are appointed.)
- Have a home inspection done to ensure the property has been maintained with integrity. (Estate representatives may not know the particulars of the home and might not be able to answer details about its condition (since they didn't own it).
- Try to find out the history on the homeowner's death, to learn whether the deceased was murdered in the home, or if he or she committed suicide. This is a touchy subject, but something like this can change the outcome of the current and future sale of that property. A murder or suicide puts a stigma on the property that will decrease the home's value in the future.
- Have a clause in place to cover any inconveniences that may arise if the estate representative was not legally allowed to sell the property (i.e.: remuneration, closing date changes, etc.) Trust me this happens a lot!
- Be very flexible and open minded for mistakes to happen on or near the closing date. Keep in mind the executor may be a loved one of the deceased, and your patience and tolerance for error will no doubt be appreciated.

Estate sales can be difficult to carry out for everyone involved, especially when there are emotions involved. Most often a lack of experience by a participant involved in the sale of the estate can result in a delayed closing and funds being held back. Mistakes are preventable, but more often than not can occur with estate property sales. Upon closing would be a great time to set up an appointment with your lawyer to include the new home in your will or to draft up a new will if you don't already have one. Do not leave your wishes to the mercy of the government upon your death.

Setting up Utilities

So your home purchase has gone firm and you have a move-in date...now what?

Timing

You may or may not be involved with a service provider or utility company at this moment. If you are in fact using a service provider, make sure to update the provider at least two weeks before your move-out date. The same goes for moving *into* your new property. With end-of-month backlog, you will want to make sure everything goes smoothly for you and that there is no disruption of service. Ask the service provider to start their service a day ahead.

Who to Use

If you are unsure about what company to use, it is best to Google the companies in the area to get information. Google is a great resource and has all the contact information right at your fingertips.

***BEWARE! There are fraudsters! Especially among the hydro/energy providers. Do not sign anything at your doorstep once you have moved in. If a man unexpectedly shows up and asks you to sign a contract, close the door and call the police and/or your local energy provider or the current provider you have signed up with. A girlfriend of mine had total chaos at her new home when she was moving in. Luckily her brothers were there to help. Two men showed up and said they were from her current hydro company. They must have caught on she was a new buyer and easy prey. They told her she had to sign the new contract (which she reluctantly did), then went in her basement and started to tear out her hot water tank. Her brother found it suspicious and called the local hydro company. They sent an employee within minutes. (Yes minutes!) That employee showed up, literally dragged the two men out of my friend's home, and threw their equipment into their van. He told them if they returned the police would be called. My girlfriend had already started her new contract with the former company and service continued without the need to change the tank or visit her home. There is a class-action lawsuit in play for the unethical business acts of the former company. The company itself was legitimate, unfortunately their actions to secure new business was not. Let's hope justice is served and new homeowners will not have to be scammed again.

Be Prepared

You may be asked to give a deposit for the new service. If you are new on their database, they want to make sure they have the security of funds in place in case you don't pay or skip town. Once you have a good payment record, or once you move at a future date they will give the deposit back. If the company is trying to win over your business (if they care enough to do so) you may be able to have the deposit waived as a bargaining tool. The service provider may also want to run a credit check, for the same reasons as above. Be prepared to get asked a lot of questions over and over again. Have a void cheque ready (some do it the old fashioned way), and have your bank prepared to fill out an Electronic Funds Transfer form for payments for the services provided.

Going Forward

Keep the utility websites bookmarked on your laptop or phone for easy access. You will also want to file the invoices properly in case there are any tax write-offs to take advantage of, or for other reasons. If you're not paying through automatic bank payment, always note the date of payment and what method you used. Always remember to check if it is done automatically.

Moving and Packing Tips

First and foremost, hire your mover as soon as you know you are moving. Reputable companies are quite busy and they may have to refer you to an affiliate company if you leave it too late.

- Gather all required packing supplies and moving boxes of different sizes.
- Make a spacious packing station at your current residence.
- Make sure to pack everything that belongs in a particular room together, in a room-labeled box.
- Pack an "Open First" box.
- Pack a suitcase or box for each member of the family several days in advance.
- Create a "Moving File" with important paperwork you will need throughout your move.
- Clean out the kitchen. Toss away junk and only box things that you use. Use your food-storage containers for all loose things you find as you empty drawers from the kitchen, desks, or table drawers.
- Begin taking apart any large items and placing all hardware in double-thick Ziploc bags, according to contents and room.
- Make sure you keep the box of hardware and tools in a central place where everyone can find it.
- Stack the boxes as you are finished filling, taping, and labeling them.
- Look in each room, and make sure that everything has been removed.
- When the truck has been filled and the movers tell you that they have everything, remember to check out each room to make sure that nothing has been left behind.

*not intended to solicit those under contract

- Always leave the home in pristine condition. No buyer likes to have to throw away your garbage and clean your mess. A buyer expects not to have to do anything but move in. Leave a good impression for the people that deemed your home "the one".

Owning a Home

not intended to solicit those under contract

Home Maintenance Plan

Ok ladies...this is the real deal here. These are the main home-maintenance tips to keep your home operating properly and efficiently. To hear a home inspector explain it can be mind boggling if you don't know what he/she is talking about. Which I admit I don't...On a good day, even after my minimum two morning coffees. I've asked the very qualified "Turbo Jim," my home inspector, to do a tour of my home to point out and explain the upkeep to maintain my home that is necessary and within reason.

Fall

Exterior:

- **Air conditioning (exterior):** The exterior component of the air conditioner is called the compressor; this is the box, with a vent and fan on top. Make sure when you are turning it off for the cold season to put on a fitted cover for weather protection. (Do not forget to remove it in the spring when you start it up again.)
- **Exterior Doors:** You should not be able to see any light through any exterior doors. If you do, seal them with weather stripping. Make sure the outside is caulked to prevent air and moisture from coming in or out.
- **Windows:** Make sure the exterior and interior are caulked and sealed to prevent air and moisture from coming in or out.
- **Eaves:** Look for debris, nails popped out, and leaks. Have eaves inspected and cleared out if they're full of debris.
- **Brick:** Look over the mortar and any new cracks that appear. If damage occurs, consult with a professional to determine the cause of the new damage. The weather could cause further cracking to occur and allow air and moisture (not to mention bugs since they typically follow moisture) into the home. This will cause further damage to the interior as well as the exterior.

not intended to solicit those under contract

- **Siding:** Make sure siding is not broken, falling off, or cracked; this allows air and moisture to enter the inside and outside of your home, which will cause damage such as mold.

- **Dryer Vent:** (Located outside near where your dryer is located inside.) Clear of any lint or debris, otherwise it could cause damage, or fire. Do not put on screens, as they trap lint.

- **Hoses:** Make sure the tap pipe is secure in the wall and there is no leaking. When shutting down for the winter, shut off the water valve inside the home and keep the outside handle to open (make sure to drain it). This prevents water from remaining, freezing, and damaging your pipes. Roll up any garden hoses, making certain they are empty of water, and store them in the garage or indoors to prevent cracking.

- **Hot Tub:** Drain and look for any debris, change filter, fill with new water. Check cover for cracks or damage.

- **Debris:** Clear up all debris from the exterior and yard. Unless you want critters to get busy making new homes and having babies in there come spring.

- **Garage:** Test door opener (if automatic) to see if it disengages via sensor when an object is directly under the door. This is mostly for the safety of children who may think it is fun to roll from under the door to get out in time. (Yes it does happen.) If the sensor is too low or not working properly it could be a crush hazard.

- **Pool:** We always recommend a professional to open and close a pool. Keep service records for future sale and warranties.

Interior:

- **Air Conditioner (interior):** Shut the air conditioner power off (at the breaker). This avoids inadvertently turning on the air conditioner, which can cause serious damage to the unit if it runs in low temperatures.

- **Attic:** Make sure you can't feel a draft coming from the attic access door (that small square that you can barely fit your body into). If you feel any heat or cold, upgrade the seal (ask your contractor).

- **Duct cleaning:** Get your ducts cleaned. It's best to do it in the fall when it is a nice temperature to leave windows open and there are fewer bugs.

Winter

Exterior:

- **Snow Removal:** Clear snow away from the foundation. (This is even more important if the foundation is not concrete.) An accumulation of snow melting and freezing will cause some materials to crack and possibly become warped. This will potentially cause moisture to enter into your home and damage the foundation. Be sure to have snow removed from the ground below any gates that access the backyard. Lack of attention to this can make for a real hassle when there's a wall of ice and snow barring your access when you need to open the gate.

- **Roof:** Watch out for sagging from the weight of snow. This could be an indication of a need for attention in the spring, when the roof might require ventilation or replacement. Note: Here in Canada, a south-facing roof typically requires replacement more often, as it is exposed to more sun than roofs exposed in other directions. Look for icicles coming down off the roof. This likely indicates that the attic is too warm and is not being vented properly. Check the attic to feel whether it is warm or cold. It should feel cool and possibly breezy if it's windy outside. You may need to call a roofing guy or contractor to remedy the problem.

- **Hot Tub:** Drain and look for any debris, change filter, and fill with new water. Check cover for cracks or damage.

Interior:

- **Attic:** (twice a year) Look at nails that hold shingles down (roofing nails) as they shouldn't be rusty. There should be no black staining around the sides of nails.

Spring

Exterior:

- **Hoses:** Make sure the pipe is secure in the wall and there is no cracking evident. Turn on the water from the inside of the home, then go to the tap on the outside and turn it on, ensuring no leaking taking place inside or outside.

- **Hot Tub:** Drain and look for any debris, change filter, and fill with new water. Check cover for cracks or damage.

- **Air Conditioner:** Remove outside cover off the compressor. Restore power (on the breaker) 48 hours before use. This will allow the compressor to warm up before starting up. Check that the compressor is still level as a change in angle can cause damage. Remove vegetation to keep it from entering the cavity. Use caution with the weed whacker as you do not want to damage the exterior. If you have any issues call a licensed HVAC technician.

Summer

Exterior:

- **Moss and sand:** Check for moss growing or sand (not soil) accumulation around the exterior of the home. This indicates either a moisture issue or lack of sunlight (or both). The absence of these can guarantee that you are not giving mold a good place to grow.
- **Wood to earth contact:** Any wood structure that is making contact with the ground should be checked regularly to check for deterioration. Wood absorbs moisture readily and can lose its strength and integrity if it's absorbing too much moisture from the earth. This is common in decks and fences.
- **Windows:** Make sure wooden windows stay painted and sealed.
- **Attic:** At least twice a year look at nails that hold shingles down (roofing nails) as they shouldn't be rusty – no black staining around sides of nails.
- **Hot Tub:** Drain and look for any debris, change filter, fill with new water. Check cover for cracks or damage.

Non-Seasonal (In other words, do it regularly.)

Exterior:

- **Steps:** No trip hazards; make sure there is a railing at all times, to remove a potential fall hazard.
- **Interlocking:** Efflorescence and sand means there is moisture pooling; land may need to be re-graded. Have it tamped regularly (landscaper).
- **Lot grading:** Look for new washout; debris being pushed toward the home indicates possible water flow in wrong direction...find out where the source is and have it corrected.
- **Gates:** Look for pinch hazards, check for squeaking, make sure they're fully operational.

- **Chimney:** Check for a screened rain cap, look for any cracks. (May need binoculars.)
- **Shingles:** Observe for curling, cracking, loose, and damaged ones.
- **Hot Tub:** Drain every 3 months at a minimum, as well as change or wash the filter (if washable). Replace the filter at least every year. It's best to have it maintained by a pool and spa professional.
- **Trees and plants:** Nothing closer than 18" to the foundation. Branches not closer than 6' from the exterior of the home. Prune often. No vines growing up the side of your home...They are cute but very damaging to the exterior.
- **Home exterior and window edges:** Check for holes and/or cracks. Do not use foam to fill...foams absorbs moisture, which will expand when frozen. Best to call an expert when it comes to filling cracks in different exteriors. What works for one may not work in another, or may damage it.
- **Driveway:** Cracks and settlement need to be sealed – they can happen quickly.
- **Garbage and Compost:** Keep as far away from the house as possible. Garbage= critters and smell.
- **Sprinklers:** Do NOT water your house – water your lawn!
- **Lawn:** Decide if this is a task you want to manage. If you are up to mowing your lawn, knock your heels off. Otherwise there are lots of hot landscapers waiting for the job. Pull weeds promptly. Re-sod dead areas and water well. Issues beyond watering and reseeding should be handled by a professional landscaper.
- **Critters:** They are so darn cute...but don't feed them unless you want to welcome the damage that comes with inviting these furry friends into your world.

Interior:

- **Ceiling:** Observe any leak, stains, or cracks and even possible sagging (as they all indicate water issues).
- **Walls:** Cracking at the point where the wall touches the ceiling on the upper level of a home is normal, unless it is severe. This is due to truss uplift (when your roof contracts and expands over time). Fill cracks and voids when necessary.
- **Interior windows and doors:** Open and close regularly to see if they are operational. Look for fog or moisture inside the pane. If observed call a professional.
- **Floors:** if ceramic, keep grout sealed and free of cracks. For other finishes, always follow manufacturer's instructions for care and repair.

- **Bathrooms:** To test if toilet is loose, cradle toilet between your legs while standing (no this is not a joke!) and try to wiggle it. If it moves it might be loose. Call a plumber before it leaks! Flush the toilet to see if there is slow drainage. This could indicate blockage in the waste line or vent stack. This could be a plumber's job or it might be a city issue. A plumber will determine which one. Tap tiles to make sure they don't sound hollow. If they do, they are no longer adhering and may indicate a leak. Make sure there are no cracks. Ensure silicone is still sealing the wet zones (i.e.: tub, sink, etc.). Dig out old silicone and replace with new. Do not go over the top of the old silicone. If your house has a septic system, test water every 6 months or more to make sure water is safe to drink. Hardware stores usually carry a water testing kit and you will need to locate your local water-testing lab for drop off.

- **Well and septic:** If you are on well water, your septic should be emptied every 5 years at a minimum. Check your pump pressure once a month, and make sure it is not running too often. If so, it may indicate a problem with the pipe; leaking. See <u>Sewers vs. Septic</u> a little later in the book for more information about septic systems.

- **Furnace room:** No combustibles. Change furnace filter once a month. Make sure carbon dioxide detectors are working.

- **Hot water tank:** Drain annually. Canadian water has dirt and calcium in it and silt builds up at the bottom of the tank. You need to shut it off and open the valve on the side so water will drain out of it.

- **Extension cords:** Not be used as a permanent electrical outlet or to travel through walls or floors.

- **Basement:** Use your senses...smell, sight... look for staining, specifically baseboards. Foundation; look for new cracks. Any damp or "off" smells can indicate mold. If you detect dampness, make sure to use a dehumidifier right away and call a remediation expert to remedy.

- **Attic:** Look at the sheathing (the plywood or wafer board that the 2×4s are attached to) for mold, moisture stains, or ice. If mold stains are apparent, call in a mold remediation expert. Attic should always be cool or cold. If it's warm or hot, air circulation is being blocked somehow, and this should be investigated. It could be as simple as soffit vents being blocked by insulation.

- **Chimney:** How often your chimney needs to be cleaned is best determined by the chimney sweeper, as fireplace usage from one household to another could vary greatly.

- **Water meter:** If the red triangle is moving, there is water flowing. If someone is not taking a shower or you are not running the sprinkler and the triangle is moving you may have a leak somewhere. If this is the case, shut off the water and call a plumber.

- **Fire alarms:** Change batteries twice a year. Pressing the button does not test the detector itself, only the battery. To actually test your fire detectors put a match or candle beneath it to set it off.

- **Appliances:** Keep up to date with "recallchek.com". Make sure the appliances are always operational and note any gas smells. Stove should ALWAYS be ventilated to the exterior of the home (controlled moisture). Clean the filter regularly for grease. Keep an eye out for leaks coming from the bottom of the fridge. If you spot any, call an appliance professional or utilize the warranty program. If a bad smell emerges from your dishwasher, have it checked by a professional. Lack of use can cause seals to get brittle and dry. Run the machine once in a while to keep them supple.

- **Gas:** If you smell gas (smells like rotten eggs) evacuate immediately. Shut off gas from the exterior meter (try to find out where it is before an emergency occurs) then call 911. Do not re-enter the home until advised it is save to do so.

- **CO:** if detector goes off, call 911 and evacuate. (Know what the detector sounds like when it goes off.)

- **Lights:** Never exceed maximum wattage. Always follow manufacturer's recommendations.

- **Electrical:** If you have aluminum (sometimes hard to determine and requires an electrician's inspection), have a licensed electrician do an initial maintenance check and decide on what needs to be done going forward. If you have fuses, make sure there are none missing (those circular "plugs") and replace with new ones of the correct amperage. Do not replace with larger amp fuses if they keep blowing, as this will not solve the problem, Instead, it may cause a fire...which is a BIGGER problem! Test your GFCI outlets (outlets with a push button in the middle, typically located in kitchens and bathrooms) by pushing the button to make sure it shuts off. (Test with a running appliance.) Outlets should always be GFCI types when near a water source.

- **Fire and Carbon Monoxide Alarms:** Change the batteries every 6 months (if not hard wired) to keep the alarms are in good working order.

If you are not comfortable checking the above items, call your home inspector. (See back for a list of preferred vendors.) They can perform a walk-through maintenance inspection annually to make sure nothing has changed that you didn't notice.

Septic Systems

A septic system can be tricky. There are guidelines you need to adhere to in order to have it run to code and to keep it in good working order. Sewage systems are more efficient and easier to run, but if the house with the septic system is the one calling your name to buy it, read on. I highly recommend hiring professionals to maintain your septic for health and safety reasons.

Part of your septic system is your "sump pump." Frequently, we homeowners don't think about our sump pumps until their no longer working and there's water damage. Once you're properly educated, there are steps you can take that will help avoid costly mishaps.

Sump Pump Maintenance Tips

Every three or four months: Put some heavy-duty gloves on and clean the pump screen or inlet opening. If your sump collects the discharge from an automatic washing machine, cleaning will be required more often. Before removing the pump, be sure to disconnect the unit from electrical power and reconnect it after completing cleaning. Then, pour enough water into the sump to cycle the pump and assure its proper functioning. Or hire a professional.

Annually: Again with the gloves...remove and clean the pump. Clean the sump pit also. Unless your pump instruction manual specifies otherwise, no lubrication or other maintenance will be necessary. If this doesn't sound appetizing either, hire a professional.

Water Alarm

You should install a water alarm (if not existing) that detects water leaks before they cause costly property damage and/or mold growth. Simple leaks from water heaters, sink drains, broken washing machine hoses, or clogged air conditioner drain tubes are immediately detected. Place an alarm wherever there is risk of water damage; utility room, laundry room, kitchen, bathroom, basement, or crawlspace.

Battery Backup Sump Pumps:

A battery-backup sump pump can help keep your basement from flooding. In the event of a power outage or mechanical failure of the AC pump, the battery-backup sump pump will begin to pump automatically.

Water Powered or Water Driven Sump Pumps:

These pumps are sometimes used in place of motor-driven sump pumps. It is important that if water powered pumps are installed they include back-flow protection devices that meet local and national plumbing codes.

Refer to a professional when dealing with your septic system. Mistakes in the maintenance and repair can lead to a very "stinky" and costly situation.

Tips:

- Know the mapping of your system. Keep all service records.
- Have the tank pumped every 3-5 years and thoroughly inspected
- Be aware of where the drain field is located; do not plant trees, shrubs or large plants on or near it. Do not park vehicles or place pools on top of it. Basically do not load weight on the field or compromise it in any way.
- Be sure that any plumbing improvements such as new toilets, extra bathrooms, etc. meet code requirements as to maintain the integrity of the system. The system is designed to bare only a certain amount of waste load and function. Adding to this load risks damaging the system and personal health of people using it.
- Check periodically for the smell of sewer gases and seeping of raw sewage.
- Be wary of what you put down the sink and in the toilets.
- Most importantly, do not use harmful chemicals or bleach in the toilets and sinks. This can affect the system and poison the surrounding area.

Home Alarms

"To arm or not to arm." Getting an alarm system is a personal choice. It may come about due to the actual reason you are leaving (personal safety) or the area you are moving to. Regardless of the reason, make sure you are making a decision based on YOUR needs, without influence of others.

There are varying kinds of alarm systems:

- Wired, wireless
- Contact sensors, motion sensors, glass breakage detectors
- Combination systems providing both fire and intrusion protection

Choosing an alarm is like choosing a phone company. What is appropriate for your needs? How safe will it make you feel? Will it truly change the outcome if someone breaks in to your home?

The price you pay will be determined by whether you are choosing just a bell system or whether you are going with the full sensors and central monitoring system. The number of windows and doors you intend to have covered will add to your cost as well.

There are a few advantages and disadvantages when adding a home alarm system.

Advantages:

- Having a system in place could save on home insurance if you choose a central monitoring system.
- Displaying the alarm company logo on the outside of the home and windows can deter a burglar from breaking in.
- If the system includes video surveillance, it can record activities that otherwise would be unknown, which can also help to catch the intruder.

not intended to solicit those under contract

Disadvantages:

- Alarm can be set off by mistake (by kids, pets, etc.), causing monitoring company to possibly penalize the homeowner.
- Can be very costly, depending on plan chosen.
- You may realize undesired entry if the wrong person knows how to disarm, or cuts phone lines.
- Codes can be easy to forget.
- When authorities are dispatched, it will take 3-4 hours unless you are able to talk over the two-way and declare a medical emergency, or have face to face contact with a burglar.
- Power outages will disengage the alarm system.
- Mixing of old systems to new systems may not work.
- You may find yourself paying for the system but never using it, for fear of tripping off the alarm.

As you can see, there are more disadvantages demonstrated. These can arise mostly from improper use. It is up to you to determine the benefits versus the drawbacks.

Choosing an Alarm Company

Choosing a company can be confusing. First, you need to determine your budget. If you need to have the contact sensors installed, there will be an initial cost for doing this. There is typically a monthly fee for the service thereafter. Get quotes from at least three companies. Afterwards, look them up on the Better Business Bureau site (http://www.bbb.org/). If you end up eliminating one or two companies based on these results, choose a couple more until you have three viable options to choose from. Call their customer service lines.
>   Are they courteous?
>   Professional?
>   Responsive?

Book an appointment with each company to have a representative come to your home and explain the service standards, response times, and operational systems they have in place to protect your home. Inquire about possible additional features, such as smoke or fire detection systems and panic buttons. This decision should not be rushed as it can be costly to change a system once you have it established.

Taking Over an Existing Alarm System

If you are considering taking over an existing system (you just bought a house) you will need to double-check that you have been given your codes, and service and system information on closing. Most user manuals should be available online if they're not provided. You will want to inquire about whether the system was in use, and if not, why? Do check the Better Business Bureau to find out if the company is on the up and up. Book an appointment with a service representative from the company to show you how the system works and to provide any updates required.

Home Emergency Kit

A disaster supplies kit is simply a collection of basic items you may need in the home in the event of an emergency. Don't assume there is someone else you can rely on to provide the things you need when you need them. Girlfriend, you need to be a provider and protector even in the toughest times. Don't leave yourself vulnerable and without amenities at a potentially volatile time.

Try to assemble your kit well in advance of any emergency taking place. You may have to evacuate at a moment's notice and take only the most important things with you. (Yes the kids first!) You will probably not have time to search for the supplies you need or to shop for them.

You may need to fend for yourself after an emergency. This means having your own food, water, and other supplies in sufficient quantity to last for several hours or days. Local officials and relief workers will be on the scene after a disaster but they cannot reach everyone immediately – hence needing to be able to manage for hours or days.

Additionally, basic services such as electricity, gas, water, sewage treatment, and telephones may be cut off for days or even a week, or longer. Your supplies kit should contain items to help you manage during these outages.

Basic Disaster Supply Kit

A basic emergency supply kit could include the following recommended items:

- Water, one gallon of water per person per day for at least three days; for drinking and sanitation
- Food, at least a three-day supply of non-perishable food
- Battery-powered or hand crank radio and a Weather Radio with tone alert and extra batteries for both
- Flashlight and extra batteries
- First-aid kit
- Whistle, to signal for help

not intended to solicit those under contract

- Dust mask to help filter contaminated air, and plastic sheeting and duct tape to shelter-in-place
- Moist towelettes, garbage bags, and plastic ties for personal sanitation
- Wrench or pliers to turn off utilities
- Manual can opener for food
- Local maps
- Cell phone with chargers, inverter, or solar charger

Extra Supplies

Once you have gathered the supplies for a basic emergency kit, you may want to consider adding the following items:

- Prescription medications and glasses
- Infant formula and diapers Pet food and extra water for your pet
- Cash and change
- Important family documents such as copies of insurance policies, identification, and bank account records in a waterproof, portable container.
- Sleeping bag or warm blanket for each person. Consider additional bedding if you live in a cold-weather climate.
- Complete change of clothing, including a long-sleeved shirt, long pants, and sturdy shoes. Consider additional clothing if you live in a cold weather climate. Household chlorine bleach and medicine dropper – When diluted, nine parts water to one part bleach, bleach can be used as a disinfectant. Or in an emergency, you can use it to treat water by using 16 drops of regular household liquid bleach per gallon of water. Do not use bleach that is scented, color safe, or with added cleaners.
- Fire extinguisher
- Matches in a waterproof container
- Feminine supplies and personal hygiene items
- Mess kits, paper cups, plates, paper towels, and plastic utensils
- Paper and pencil
- Books, games, puzzles, or other activities for children

First Aid Kit

In any emergency a family member or you, yourself, may suffer an injury. If you have these basic first aid supplies you are better prepared to help your loved ones when they are hurt.

Knowing how to treat minor injuries can make a difference in an emergency. You might consider taking a first aid class, but simply having the following things can help you stop bleeding, prevent infection, and assist in decontamination.

- Two pairs of Latex gloves, or other sterile gloves if you are allergic to Latex
- Sterile dressings to stop bleeding
- Cleansing agent/soap and antibiotic towelettes
- Antibiotic ointment
- Burn ointment
- Adhesive bandages in a variety of sizes
- Eye wash solution to flush the eyes or as general decontaminant
- Thermometer
- Asthma inhalers or prescription medications you take every day such as insulin or heart medicine. You should periodically rotate medicines to account for expiration dates.
- Prescribed medical supplies such as glucose and blood pressure monitoring equipment and supplies

Non-prescription drugs:

- Aspirin or non-aspirin pain reliever
- Anti-diarrhea medication
- Antacid
- Laxative

Other first aid supplies:

- Scissors
- Tweezers
- Tube of petroleum jelly or other lubricant

Unique Needs

Remember the unique needs of your family members, including growing children, when making your emergency supply kit and family emergency plan.

For Baby:

- Formula
- Diapers
- Bottles
- Powdered milk
- Medications
- Moist towelettes
- Diaper rash ointment

For Adults:

- Denture needs
- Contact lenses and supplies
- Extra eye glasses

Ask your doctor about storing prescription medications such as heart and high blood pressure medication, insulin, and other prescription drugs.

If you live in a cold climate, you must think about warmth. It is possible that you will not have heat. Think about your clothing and bedding supplies. Be sure to include one complete change of clothing and shoes per person, including:

- Jacket or coat
- Long pants
- Long-sleeved shirt

Food

Consider the following things when putting together your emergency food supplies:

- Store at least a three-day supply of non-perishable food.
- Choose foods your family will eat.
- Remember any special dietary needs.

- Avoid foods that will make you thirsty.
- Choose salt-free crackers, whole grain cereals, and canned foods with high liquid content.

Following a disaster, there may be power outages that could last for several days. Stock canned foods, dry mixes, and other staples that do not require refrigeration, cooking, water, or special preparation. Be sure to include a manual can opener and eating utensils.

Ideal Emergency Food Supplies

The following items are suggested when selecting emergency food supplies. You may already have many of these on hand.

- Ready-to-eat canned meats, fruits, vegetables, and a can opener
- Protein or fruit bars, dry cereal or granola
- Peanut butter
- Dried fruit
- Nuts
- Crackers
- Canned juices
- Non-perishable pasteurized milk
- High energy foods
- Vitamins
- Food for infants
- Comfort/stress foods

Food Safety

Flood, fire, national disaster, or the loss of power from high winds, snow or ice could jeopardize the safety of your food. Knowing what to do before and after an emergency can help you reduce your risk of illness and minimize the amount of food that may be lost due to spoilage.

Power outages can occur at any time of the year, and it may take from a few hours to several days for electricity to be restored to residential areas. Without electricity or a cold source, food stored in refrigerators and freezers can become unsafe. Bacteria in food grow rapidly at temperatures between 4 and 60°Celcius, and if these foods are consumed, people can become very sick.

Do:

- Keep food in covered containers.
- Keep cooking and eating utensils clean.
- Keep garbage in closed containers and dispose outside, burying garbage if necessary.
- Keep your hands clean by washing them frequently with soap and water that has been boiled or disinfected.
- Discard any food that has come into contact with contaminated floodwater.
- Discard any food that has been at room temperature for two hours or more.
- Discard any food that has an unusual odour, color, or texture.
- Use ready-to-feed formula, if possible, for formula-fed infants. If using ready-to-feed formula is not possible, it is best to use bottled water to prepare powdered or concentrated formula. If bottled water is not available, use boiled water. Use treated water to prepare formula only if you do not have bottled or boiled water. Breastfed infants should continue breastfeeding.

Don't:

- Eat foods from cans that are swollen, dented, or corroded, even though the product may look safe to eat.
- Eat any food that looks or smells abnormal, even if the can looks normal.
- Let garbage accumulate inside, for both fire and sanitation reasons.

Note: Thawed food usually can be eaten if it is still "refrigerator cold." It can be re-frozen if it still contains ice crystals. To be safe, remember, "When in doubt, throw it out."

Cooking

Alternative cooking sources in times of emergency including candle warmers, chafing dishes, fondue pots or a fireplace.
Charcoal grills and camp stoves are for outdoor use only.
Commercially canned food may be eaten out of the can without warming.
To heat food in a can:

1. Remove the label.
2. Thoroughly wash and disinfect the can. (Use a diluted solution of one part bleach to ten parts water.)
3. Open the can before heating.

Managing Food without Power

Be Prepared:

- Have a refrigerator thermometer.
- Know where you can get dry ice.
- Keep a few days' worth of ready-to-eat foods on hand that do not require cooking or cooling.

When the Power Goes Out:

- Keep the refrigerator and freezer doors closed as much as possible.
- The refrigerator will keep food cold for about 4 hours if it is unopened.
- Refrigerators should be kept at 4° Celsius or below for proper food storage.

Once the Power is restored:

- Check the temperature inside the refrigerator and freezer.
- If an appliance thermometer was kept in the freezer, check the temperature when the power comes back on. If the freezer thermometer reads 4° Celsius or below, the food is safe and may be refrozen. If a thermometer has not been kept in the freezer, check each package of food to determine its safety. You can't rely on appearance or odour. If the food still contains ice crystals or is 4° Celsius or below, it is safe to refreeze or cook.
- Refrigerated food should be safe as long as the power was out for no more than 4 hours. Keep the door closed as much as possible.
- Discard any perishable food (such as meat, poultry, fish, eggs or leftovers) that has been above Celsius for two hours or more.

Using Dry Ice:

- Under normal circumstances you should not keep dry ice in your freezer. If your freezer is functioning properly it will cause the unit to become too cold and your freezer may shut off. However, if you lose power for an extended period of time, dry ice is the best way to keep things cold.
- Twenty-five pounds of dry ice will keep a 10-cubic-foot freezer below freezing for 3-4 days.
- If you use dry ice to keep your food cold, make sure it does not come in direct contact with the food.
- Use care when handling dry ice; wear dry, heavy gloves to avoid injury.

Water Supply

Water is an essential element to survival and a necessary item in an emergency supplies kit. Following a disaster, clean drinking water may not be available. Your regular water source could be cut-off or compromised through contamination. Prepare yourself by building a supply of water that will meet your family's needs during an emergency.

How Much Water Do You Need?

You should store at least one gallon of water per person per day. A normally active person needs at least one gallon of water daily just for drinking, however, individual needs vary, depending on age, physical condition, activity, diet and climate. To determine your water needs, take the following into account:

- One gallon of water per person per day, for drinking and sanitation.
- Children, nursing mothers, and sick people may need more water.
- A medical emergency might require additional water.
- If you live in a warm weather climate more water may be necessary. In very hot temperatures, water needs can double.
- Keep at least a three-day supply of water per person.

How Should You Store Water?

It is recommended you purchase commercially bottled water, in order to prepare the safest and most reliable emergency water supply. Keep bottled water in its original container and do not open until you need to use it. Observe the expiration or "use by" date. Store the water in a cool, dark place.

Preparing Your Own Water Containers

It is recommended you purchase food-grade water storage containers.
   Before filling them with water, thoroughly clean the containers with dishwashing soap and water, and rinse completely so there is no residual soap.
   If you choose to use your own storage containers, use two-liter, plastic soft drink bottles – not plastic jugs or cardboard containers that have had milk or fruit juice in them. Milk protein and fruit sugars cannot be adequately removed from these containers and provide an environment for bacterial growth when water is stored in them. Cardboard containers also leak easily and are not designed for long-term storage of liquids. Also, do not use glass containers, because they can break and are heavy.

Essentials of Water Management

Allow people to drink according to their needs.

Many people need even more than the average of one gallon per day. The individual amount needed depends on age, physical activity, physical condition and time of year. Never ration drinking water unless ordered to do so by authorities.

Drink the amount you need today and try to find more for tomorrow. Under no circumstances should a person drink less than one quart (four cups) of water each day. You can minimize the amount of water your body needs by reducing activity and staying cool.

First drink water that you know is not contaminated. If necessary, suspicious water, such as cloudy water from regular faucets, or water from streams or ponds, can be used after it has been treated. If water treatment is not possible, put off drinking suspicious water as long as possible, but do not become dehydrated.

Do not drink carbonated beverages instead of water. Carbonated beverages do not meet drinking-water requirements. Caffeinated drinks and alcohol dehydrate the body, which increases the need for drinking water.

Turn off the main water valves. If you hear reports of broken water or sewage lines or if local officials advise you of a problem, you will need to protect the water sources already in your home from contamination, To close the incoming water source, locate the incoming valve and turn it to the closed position. Be sure you and your family members know how to perform this important procedure.

Safe Water Sources

Safe Sources:

- Melted ice cubes.
- Liquids from canned goods such as fruit or vegetables.
- Water drained from pipes. To use the water in your pipes, let air into the plumbing by turning on the faucet in your home at the highest level. A small amount of water will trickle out. Then obtain water from the lowest faucet in the home.
- Water drained from the water heater. To use water in your hot-water tank, be sure the electricity or gas is off and open the drain at the bottom of the tank. Start the water flowing by turning off the water intake valve at the tank and turning on the hot-water faucet. After you are notified that clean water has been restored, you will need to refill the tank before turning the gas or electricity back on. If the gas is turned off, a professional will be needed to turn it back on.

Unsafe Sources

- Radiators, hot water boilers (home heating systems).
- Water from the toilet bowl or flush tank.
- Water beds. Fungicides added to the water or chemicals in the vinyl may make water unsafe to use.
- Swimming pools and spas. Chemicals used to kill germs are too concentrated for safe drinking, but the water can be used for personal hygiene, cleaning, and related uses.

Water Treatment

If you have used all of your stored water and there are no other reliable clean water sources, it may become necessary in an emergency situation to treat suspicious water. Treat all water of uncertain quality before using it for drinking, food washing or preparation, washing dishes, brushing teeth, or making ice. In addition to having a bad odour and taste, contaminated water can contain microorganisms (germs) that cause diseases such as dysentery, cholera, typhoid, and hepatitis.

There are many ways to treat water. None is perfect. Often the best solution is a combination of methods. Before treating, let any suspended particles settle to the bottom, or strain them through coffee filters or layers of clean cloth. Make sure you have the necessary materials in your disaster supplies kit for the chosen water treatment method.

Boiling:

Boiling is the safest method of treating water. In a large pot or kettle, bring water to a rolling boil for one full minute, keeping in mind that some water will evaporate. Let the water cool before drinking.

Boiled water will taste better if you put oxygen back into it by pouring the water back and forth between two clean containers. This also will improve the taste of stored water.

Chlorination:

You can use household liquid bleach to kill microorganisms. Use only regular household liquid bleach that contains 5.25 to 6.0 percent sodium hypochlorite. Do not use scented bleaches, color safe bleaches, or bleaches with added cleaners. Because the potency of bleach diminishes with time, use bleach from a newly opened or unopened bottle.

Add sixteen drops (1/8 teaspoon) of bleach per gallon of water stir and let stand for thirty minutes. The water should have a slight bleach odour. If it doesn't, then repeat the dosage and let stand another 15 minutes. If it still does not smell of chlorine, discard it and find another source of water.

Other chemicals, such as iodine or water treatment products sold in camping or surplus stores that do not contain 5.25 or 6.0 percent sodium hypochlorite as the only active ingredient, are not recommended and should not be used.

Distillation:

While boiling and chlorination will kill most microbes in water, distillation will remove microbes (germs) that resist these methods, as well as heavy metals, salts, and most other chemicals. Distillation involves boiling water and then collecting the vapour that condenses. The condensed vapour will not include salt or most other impurities.

To distil, fill a pot halfway with water.

Tie a cup to the handle on the pot's lid so that the cup will hang right-side-up when the lid is upside-down (make sure the cup is not dangling into the water), place the upside-down lid on the pot, and boil the water for twenty minutes. The water that drips from the lid into the cup is distilled.

Distillation is the most effective way to treat water. It kills microbes and removes contaminants (heavy metals, salts, and most other chemicals).

Fire Emergency

Make a Fire Escape Plan

No one wants to realize the disastrous effects of a fire. In the event of a one, remember that every second counts, so you and your family must always be prepared. Escape plans help you get out of your home quickly.

Twice each year, practice your home fire-escape plan. Some tips to consider when preparing this plan include:

- Find two ways to get out of each room.
- If the primary way is blocked by fire or smoke, you will need a second way out. A secondary route might be a window onto a neighbouring roof or a collapsible ladder for escape from upper story windows.
- Make sure that windows are not stuck, screens can be taken out quickly, and that security bars can be properly opened.
- Practice feeling your way out of the house in the dark or with your eyes closed.
- Windows and doors with security bars must have quick release devices to allow them to be opened immediately in an emergency. Make sure everyone in the family understands and practices how to properly operate and open locked or barred doors and windows.
- Teach children not to hide from firefighters.

Fire Alarms

A properly installed and maintained smoke alarm is the only thing in your home that can alert you and your family to a fire twenty-four hours a day, seven days a week.

A working smoke alarm significantly increases your chances of surviving a deadly home fire.

Install both ionization and photoelectric smoke alarms, or dual sensor smoke alarms, which contain both ionization and photoelectric smoke sensors.

- Test batteries monthly.
- Replace batteries in battery-powered and hard-wired smoke alarms at least once a year (except non-replaceable ten-year lithium batteries)
- Install smoke alarms on every level of your home, including the basement. Always follow the manufacturer's installation instructions when installing smoke alarms.
- Replace the entire smoke alarm unit every eight to ten years or according to manufacturer's instructions.
- Never disable a smoke alarm while cooking – it can be a deadly mistake. Open a window or door and press the "hush" button, wave a towel at the alarm to clear the air, or move the entire alarm several feet away from the location.

Fire Safety for People with Needs

- Caregivers are encouraged to check the smoke alarms of those who are unable to do it themselves.
- Audible alarms for visually impaired people should pause with a small window of silence between each successive cycle so that they can listen to instructions or for the voices of others.
- Smoke alarms with a vibrating pad or flashing light are available for the hearing impaired. Contact your local fire department for information about obtaining a flashing or vibrating smoke alarm.
- Smoke alarms with a strobe light outside the home to catch the attention of neighbours, and emergency call systems for summoning help, are also available.

Final Tips

- Sleep with your door closed.
- Only those trained in the proper use and maintenance of fire extinguishers should consider using them when appropriate.
- Contact your local fire department for information on training in your area and what kind of extinguisher to buy for your home.
- Consider installing an automatic fire sprinkler system in your residence.

Christine Denty

- Ask your local fire department to inspect your residence for fire safety and prevention.
- Visit your local fire department for up-to-date escape tips and advice.

Pests

Dealing with 2, 4, 6, 8+++ legged intruders can be nerve-racking. The very thought sends shivers up my spine.

What damage can be caused by not controlling pest invasion on your property?

- Chewed electrical and cable wires (costly to fix!)
- Chewed garden sheds.
- Burrowed and damaged grounds.
- Debris collection under porches, around exterior of the home, chimneys, etc.
- Animal waste (particularly with birds), which can damage the roof, and exterior finishes.
- Additions to the family (babies).
- Danger to humans and your domestic animals.
- Damage to interior and exterior of the home.
- Disgruntled neighbours (due to their having to tolerate your new wild friends).

Dealing with Pests:

The best game plan is prevention. Seal up any holes that don't belong and investigate the areas around your home every spring and fall. Accumulation of waste near or on the property creates a perfect breeding ground for unwanted pests. Gardens and food-providing plants can be a wonderful thing, especially for hungry pests. Be sure to have adequate fencing...while fences may not be attractive, they are the surest way to keep dogs, cats, deer, groundhogs, and other large animals out of your gardens. For deer, encircle plants with six-foot-tall (1.8 m) cages that reach several feet above the tips of the farthest branches. As to bird feeders...where do I begin with this...you will attract birds, yes! But also squirrels and rodents!

Look for Wall Penetrations:

Search for gaps between anything that passes into your walls, such as gas lines, plumbing and air conditioning lines, phone and television cables and exhaust vents.

Inspect Siding:

Gaps and holes in siding and around trim are easy to spot. Look under the siding where it meets the foundation. Rot, foundation shifting, and sloppy building practices can leave openings that pests can get through.

Inspect Doors and Windows:

Look for damaged screens and worn-out caulking or weather stripping as this might provide a way for bugs and mice to come in. Make sure the rubber gasket under your garage door seals tightly to the floor. (Replace the gasket if it doesn't seal.)

Inspect your Foundation:

Look for foundation-settling cracks in masonry, and make sure basement windows are closed and sealed tightly. If there's a crawlspace under your house, all the floors above the space are potential entry zones. If the crawlspace has an entry, put on safety glasses, crawl inside and inspect it (with a flashlight). Or better yet, bribe someone to go in there for you! A heavy concentration of cobwebs can indicate an entry point.

Inspect Exhaust Fans and Dryer Vents:

Be sure that dampers (vertical slates going across the opening) open and close freely. A sticking damper could stay open and leave a welcoming entrance for many critters, including squirrels and birds.

Inspect Roof and Soffits:

Look for holes and gaps in soffits[1] and fascia,[2] especially where they run into adjoining rooflines. These are favourite entry-points for squirrels, bats, wasps, hornets, etc.

---

1   Soffits: The exposed surface under the overhanging section of an eave.

2   Fascia: A vertical finishing edge connected to the ends of the rafters, trusses, or gutters.

Add Chimney Caps:

Chimney caps prevent birds, mice, chipmunks, squirrels and even raccoons from making the firebox of your fireplace their home.

Inspect Vents on the Roof:

Check to see that screens are not chewed-through or missing on the roof vents, because this can let squirrels or bats into your attic. EEK!

Cut Back or Remove Plants, Foliage, or Wood Piles:

Anything close to or touching your house can provide a freeway for bugs. Tree branches can spell trouble even if they're high above the ground level. Ants that feed on aphids in trees use branches as bridge access to your house. Trim back the branches to avoid this.

Ensure Gutters are Clear:

Gutters filled with debris are a great nesting spot for corn ants and other pests.

How to Deal with Neighbours (Good and Bad)

Having neighbours, for most of us, is a way of life. Just like kids in the sand box, we all have to learn to get along and share the external space around us.

The key to having peace amongst you and your neighbours is: COMMUNICATION.

Good communication can make or break the relationships you have with your neighbours. How you get the message across matters too. Some homeowners live in a fantasy neighbourhood where all the neighbours get along and invite each other over for barbecues and birthdays. To those suburban champions – kudos and congrats. Now let's address those of you who may *not* have such a good, neighbourly experience...

Neighbourly Issues

Some issues you may have to deal with are:

- noise or light disturbances.
- drug dealing or other odd activities.
- cigarette smoke or other distasteful smells creeping into your living space.
- vandalism and/or property damage.
- harassment.
- trespassing.
- your neighbour is just being straight weird: nudity, bad singing, habits that drive you nuts, etc.

You will want to find out if the disorderly conduct or disturbance breaks a municipal by-law. You can locate your local by-laws online or you can visit your City Hall to get a list of by-laws for your area.

not intended to solicit those under contract

How to handle these issues is as important as the issues themselves. As the saying goes, you get more flies with honey than with vinegar. You must give the benefit of the doubt initially, and hope that your neighbours will be receptive and open to your concerns. For all you know, you might get along quite nicely and they could simply have been oblivious to the disturbance they have created.

Here is a list (in order of how you should deal with not-so-neighbourly neighbours).

- First, document the issue. This will help you see for yourself whether it is a common occurrence, and serious or harmless. You may see the map of issues and come up with a solution on your own, just by observing the patterns that arise. The other reason to document this, is in case it gets ugly. Yes, ugly. God forbid you have to go to court – having this documentation right from the start will prove invaluable. Note any witnesses to the issue or actions of the neighbour.

- Go talk to your neighbour. Keep an open mind. If they disagree or get confrontational, then hold off and try them again the next day. Sometimes people don't take to criticism well. If they are not receptive, then you must take more formal action. If you live in a condominium, write a formal complaint to the condo board and the board members will likely address the situation with the neighbour. They do not take to the disturbance of others' enjoyment well. They have options for remediation that may satisfy you and the other owners with whom you're in conflict. But having proper documentation of the disturbance is key.

- Contact a lawyer. Having a lawyer point out the possible damages can sometimes deter the conduct, or it can escalate it, depending on how the complaint is portrayed to the neighbour. This action should be considered carefully.

- If these measures have no effect, you may need to contact police. This kinda bites, because not only will you look like a squealer, the police will take their sweet time showing up. But the police do not want things to escalate. They are aware that these are the very things out of which some unnecessary crimes can arise. Hence they'll want to put the fire out before it begins. Your neighbour won't be thrilled, but chances are, you are not the only one being inconvenienced by their actions.

- If damage, grief, loss of work, or a need for repairs is caused by the conduct of your neighbour, you should look at going to Small Claims Court (if damages are under $10,000). This is the extreme to handling this, but at times you may not have any choice in the matter.

- If this doesn't work – last resort...move. It sucks but sometimes there is no other choice. Hiring a hit man is illegal so that is not an option.

Taxation and Write-Offs

Home-Based Businesses

"Oh Canada…" Our government loves to tax us. It's good to know what you can get back into your pocket as a homeowner running a home-based business. You can use some of your home maintenance and home ownership costs as business tax deductions, which have no maximum. Generally, however, the rules for business tax deductions for home-based businesses are the same as for any other business. There are many limitations to this, (which you should discuss with your accountant), but being aware that you can get money back is the key. First of all, you must operate a legitimate business. Secondly, you must ensure that zoning regulations allow this in your municipality. You can visit your municipality's Town Office, to see what the provisions are regarding a home-based business. Your Town Office may also require that you get zoning permits for any structural changes you are making to the property for your business or office.

Some of the typical guidelines for writing off expenses on a home-based business are that outside storage must be specific (e.g.: a landscaper can write off a garage if equipment is stored there, but a hairdresser cannot). Also, the intended use of the home (per zoning) cannot be changed completely. In other words, you can't run a salon in the whole home. You can only a percentage of the home, and must still use the rest as a family residence. No structural changes are permitted to allow for a home business, such as creating extra parking, etc.

Once you have determined that you are permitted to use part of your home for a business or home-based office, it needs to be noted that this is not a license to write-off everything you buy or do. If your home-based business is making money, you need to determine whether it is your main source of income. If you earn $30,000 or more in the business, you need to submit the HST and lots of other fun things. An in-depth discussion with your accountant would be a wise move if you are looking for the extra write-offs. The last thing you want to experience is being audited and having the government impose penalties because you were not entitled to the write-offs in the first place.

not intended to solicit those under contract

Write-offs for an Investment Property

You may own a second property from which you gain rental income. These are some of the write-offs you can enjoy if the entire property is a rental:

- Mortgage interest
- Property taxes
- Insurance
- Maintenance
- Renovation upgrades (refer to your accountant about "capital cost allowance")
- Property management
- Utility bills (if you include them in the rent)
- Internet connection, telephone, cell phone

When it comes time to sell your investment property, the government will charge you tax (at your tax bracket) on fifty percent of your capital gain, (the increased value from the time you purchased the property). It is good to get the benefits of the write-offs to offset the adjusted cost base, due to improvements. In other words, your asset (the house) inherits costs when it comes to improvements, etc. Hence, the cost to acquiring that property is higher. This will narrow the capital gain realized, as the cost of improving the property eats into the overall gain. Here's how you can calculate the Adjusted Cost Base, to determine the true cost of your investments for capital gains and losses:

ACB: "ADJUSTED COST BASE"

Home purchased for: $200,000 (book value)

Reno costs: $40,000 ($240,000 = adjusted cost base – "ACB")

Home sold for $300,000 in 3 years

Total taxable gain: $60,000 ($300,000 - $240,000)

Only 50% of the $60,000 is taxable = $30,000 taxable at your tax rate. If your tax rate is 30%, $10,000 will be subject to taxation.

Always consult with a professional when it comes to owning a property and taxation. Doing it legitimately and properly has its rewards.

To Renovate or Not to Renovate

I had the opportunity to discuss renovating with Preet Banerjee, a finance expert here in Toronto. His focus is to help income earners here in Canada make the most of their dollars today, and in the future. We co-wrote an article in the *Globe and Mail* and this chapter is basically derived straight from that 2012 article, which states such a valid point: If it ain't broken, I'm not going to change it much....

We live in the generation of the renovation. Granite countertop upgrades, hardwood-floor installations, a wall removal here, some *feng shui* there. There are so many television shows centred on renovations that you might start to feel abnormal if you aren't doing something to your home. Then again, with so many people living at or beyond their means, why would you want to be normal?

There are two major reasons why you would want to renovate your home: You want to improve your living space, or you are making an investment that will increase the value of your home above and beyond the cost of the renovation. My beef is with people who use the latter reason to justify being financially irresponsible.

Don't get me wrong, I don't have anything against upgrading your living space, even if you don't get a positive return on your investment. You just need to be able to afford it, and it would be nice if it didn't end your relationship, either.

For example, perhaps you are looking at an extensive upgrade to your condo. You need to consider the factors that affect your condo's value: "If the value of the condo has been established by the neighbourhood, amount of space offered, and/or amenities provided by the condo corporation, renovating may not be as important a factor in achieving desired return as market timing would be."

If the condo is located in a "hot" area, where demand is greater than supply, renovating would be a waste of money since location is going to be what sells the property.

But let's say your $50,000 renovation increases the value of your home by $75,000. That's a total return of fifty percent on your investment. That's great if you're a flipper, but what if you're living in that home for ten more years? Your annualized rate of return is only 4.14 percent – and that assumes the upgrade you made is as desirable ten years from now as it is today. Tastes change. Maybe people will think it's hideous in a decade, in which case your reno may actually hurt you.

You are also forgoing the use of that $50,000. If you borrowed it, your cash flow is tied up paying it off. If you paid for it in cash, you have to weigh the opportunity cost – what might you have earned if you had invested the money instead?

So like I said, I don't care if you renovate. Your new environment may bring you great pleasure and pride, and that's great. If you can afford it, go nuts.

But if it puts a strain on your finances, don't fall into the trap of justifying it because it's an investment, when you really just want to keep up with the Joneses.

Selling your Home

not intended to solicit those under contract

Seller's Timeline

This chapter will cover everything you need to know as a home seller (AKA vendor). Review the timeline to have an idea as to what steps you need to conquer and when. Your sale will go smoother and be more successful when you are a few steps ahead.

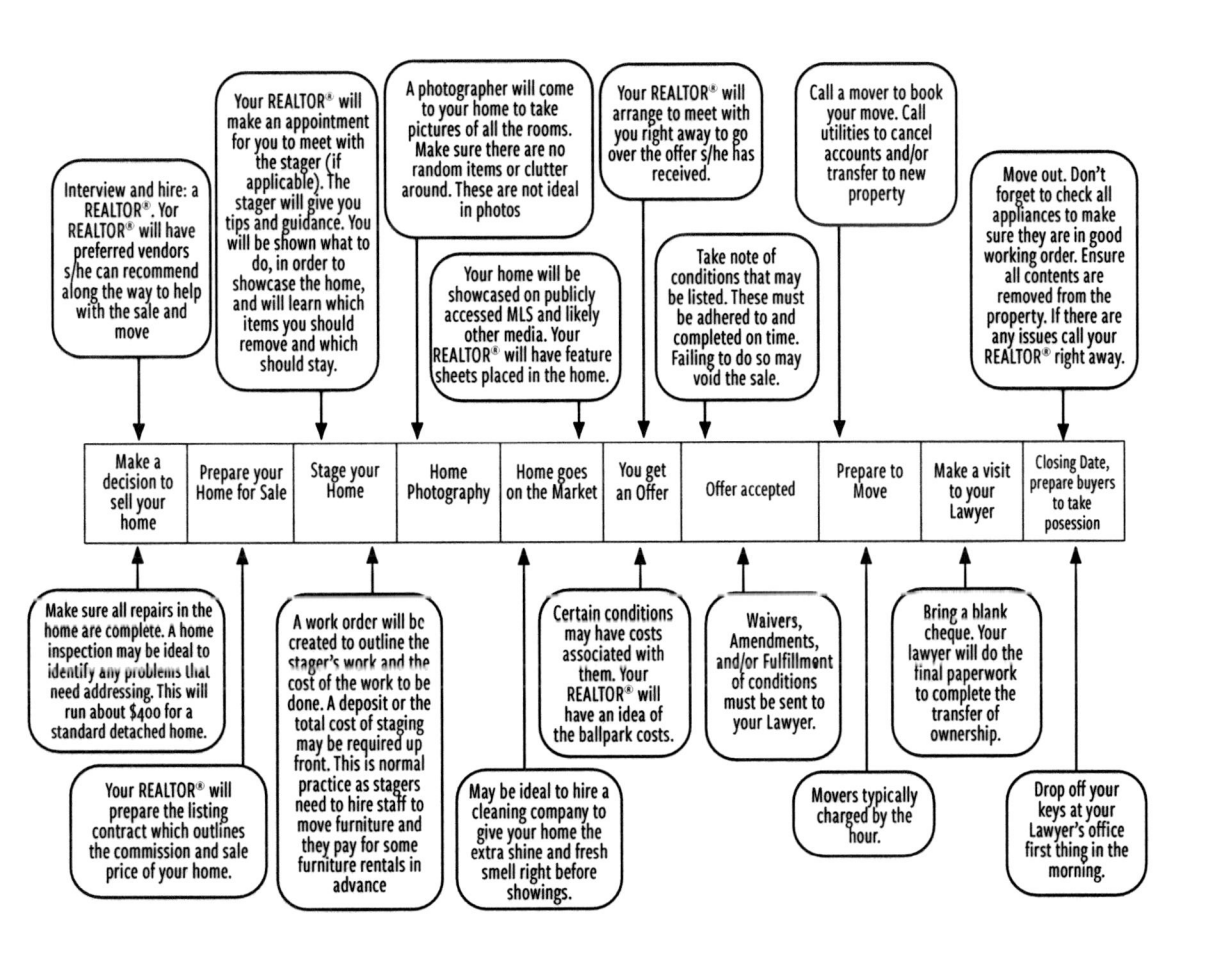

Timeline Steps

1. Make a decision to sell your home
- Interview and hire: a REALTOR®. Yor REALTOR® will have preferred vendors s/he can recommend along the way to help with the sale and move
- Make sure all repairs in the home are complete. A home inspection may be ideal to identify any problems that need addressing. This will run about $400 for a standard detached home.
- Your REALTOR® will prepare the listing contract which outlines the commission and sale price of your home.

2. Prepare your Home for Sale
- Your REALTOR® will make an appointment for you to meet with the stager (if applicable). The stager will give you tips and guidance. You will be shown what to do, in order to showcase the home, and will learn which items you should remove and which should stay.

3. Stage your Home
- A work order will be created to outline the stager's work and the cost of the work to be done. A deposit or the total cost of staging may be required up front. This is normal practice as stagers need to hire staff to move furniture and they pay for some furniture rentals in advance

4. Home Photography
- A photographer will come to your home to take pictures of all the rooms. Make sure there are no random items or clutter around. These are not ideal in photos

5. Home goes on the Market
- Your home will be showcased on publicly accessed MLS and likely other media. Your REALTOR® will have feature sheets placed in the home.
- May be ideal to hire a cleaning company to give your home the extra shine and fresh smell right before showings.

6. You get an Offer
- Certain conditions may have costs associated with them. Your REALTOR® will have an idea of the ballpark costs.

7. Offer accepted
- Your REALTOR® will arrange to meet with you right away to go over the offer s/he has received.
- Take note of conditions that may be listed. These must be adhered to and completed on time. Failing to do so may void the sale.
- Waivers, Amendments, and/or Fulfillment of conditions must be sent to your Lawyer.

8. Prepare to Move
- Call a mover to book your move. Call utilities to cancel accounts and/or transfer to new property
- Movers typically charged by the hour.

9. Make a visit to your Lawyer
- Bring a blank cheque. Your lawyer will do the final paperwork to complete the transfer of ownership.

10. Closing Date, prepare buyers to take posession
- Move out. Don't forget to check all appliances to make sure they are in good working order. Ensure all contents are removed from the property. If there are any issues call your REALTOR® right away.
- Drop off your keys at your Lawyer's office first thing in the morning.

not intended to solicit those under contract

IMPORTANT CONTACTS:

Professionals Hired:	Phone #'s	Email
REALTOR®		
Contractor:		
Stager:		
Lawyer:		
Mover:		

DATES TO REMEMBER:

Detail	Date	Date
Condition fulfillment dates:		
Home inspection date:		
Extra visit dates:		
Lawyer's appointments		
Mortgage Lender appointments:		

not intended to solicit those under contract

Knowing the Real Estate Market before Selling your Home

A successful home sale starts with careful planning and knowledge of the local and recent home market sales. Choose your REALTOR® early, so you can receive some insight on the recent home sales in your area. One of the key factors to understanding when to sell your home is that the MARKET determines what your home will sell for. You can affix any price you wish, but buyers know what other similar homes are selling for (because they are seeing them, and you are not).You may hear your REALTOR® say "Your home is only worth what the market will bear." This means your home sale-price is determined by the market. Conversely, we have seen a "seller's" market, in which sellers are experiencing several buyers bidding for their homes. This is a seller's dream come true.

   I have had sellers tell me that they need the home to sell for a certain amount, and then they price it accordingly. Folks, this does not work if you are pricing your home for more than a buyer will pay for it. It may even put you at risk of even greater losses if it sits on the market too long and appears unwanted.

*not intended to solicit those under contract

The Girlfriend's Fabulous Guide to Real Estate

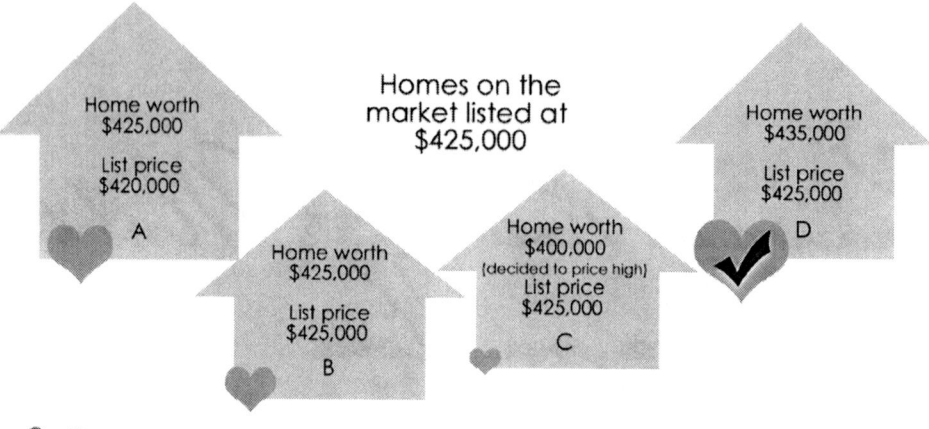

Homes on the market listed at $425,000

A — Home worth $425,000 / List price $420,000

B — Home worth $425,000 / List price $425,000

C — Home worth $400,000 (decided to price high) / List price $425,000

D — Home worth $435,000 / List price $425,000 ✓

Buyers Norma and Mike have a budget of $440,000 to buy a home. Today they are looking at homes in the $425,000+ price range. Home C is the least desired as it does not compare well to the others they have seen today. It is scratched off their consideration list.

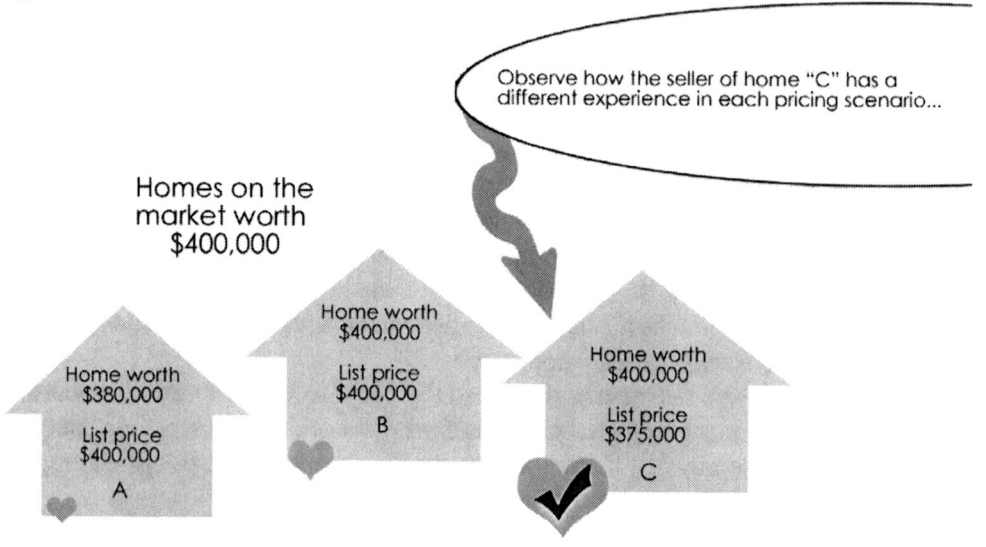

Observe how the seller of home "C" has a different experience in each pricing scenario...

Homes on the market worth $400,000

A — Home worth $380,000 / List price $400,000

B — Home worth $400,000 / List price $400,000

C — Home worth $400,000 / List price $375,000 ✓

Buyers Julia and David have a budget of $420,000 to buy a home. Today they are looking at homes in the $400,000 price range. They feel home C is superior to the others they have seen today. Other buyers who viewed the home today felt the same. Given that Julia and David believe they will not be the only ones trying to buy this house, they offer more than the asking price to make sure they win the bid.. The home ends up selling for $415,000 because buyers feel it has shown better than it's competition.

The state of the economy plays a very big role in the outcome of the sale of your home. REALTORS® do not have a crystal ball. They can give insight on the possible outcome, but no one knows what the end result will be until an offer is accepted. Any forward knowledge is merely speculation on anyone's part. Your REALTOR® can pull up past sales' info to show you what the last month or several months have looked like for your area.

December Average selling price by Housing Type ($)

AREA	AVG. PRICE	SINGLE DETACHED	SEMI-DETACHED	CONDO/ TOWNHOUSE	CONDO APT.	LINK	ATTACHED ROW
DURHAM	451,671	508,833	355,297	290,839	271,003	391,482	407,089
AJAX	507,035	577,997	469,275	323,055	336,625	367,000	434,734
BROCK	395,914	395,914	-	317,500	-	-	-
CLARINGTON	433,924	496,545	323,725	239,200	225,100	376,429	308,500
OSHAWA	357,155	397,497	293,101	213,467	178,850	355,333	256,167
PICKERING	514,039	649,518	428,100	326,075	338,650	450,000	447,000
SCUGOG	437,292	449,942	285,500	402,000	-	-	-
UXBRIDGE	875,967	875,967	-	621,490	-	-	-
WHITBY	481,197	544,537	362,450	293,375	297,513	429,607	404,894

Per Durham Region Association of REALTORS® December 2015 Market Update Report

Luxury Homes

Certain types of homes are more popular than others. Newer homes tend to have a larger market, as they don't typically need many repairs or updates. More importantly though, the price point of the home may (or may not) serve a large demographic. If your home is in the $1,000,000+ market, you may find that it takes longer to sell. This is not because it is too big, but merely because the few buyers that actually are in the market for a luxury home will be very picky and they do shop around. If the inventory for luxury homes happens to be low, you may be fortunate that an anxious buyer will buy it quickly, but that is the best-case scenario. Your REALTOR® needs to know how to market your home, in order to get the traffic it needs for a faster and more profitable sale.

"Diamonds are a girl's best friend..."

$1,000,000+
Mostly the filthy rich. Least popular demographic, making up only 2% of the economy and in some areas almost non-existent. Home value very difficult to dicipher as typically custom built. Special measures required to prepare and sell these homes

$700,000 - $990,000
Less popular and serves only a niche market, fewer of this demographic in the economy, home value is difficult to decipher as variances exist (custom homes, differences in interior elements)

$550,000-$690,000
Popular and saleable, evident density of this demographic in the economy
-Middle to high income family

$400,000-$540,000
Most popular and saleable, highest density of this demographic in the economy
-Middle income family

$250,000-$390,000
Popular and saleable, evident density of this demographic in the economy
-Low to middle income family

$150,000-$249,000
Less popular, home requires work, entrance level into home ownership demographic may not commonly qualify for financing. Property investors usually seek these properties
-Low and/or single income family

$0-$150,000
Very rare sale, typically not financeable
-Very low or single income family

To further this knowledge, I have included a report from our government website that shows "Median Total Income." This shows what our population's most popular salary range is. Knowing this helps to determine your home's affordability to buyers in today's market.

	2009	2010	2011	2012	2013
	all census families[1]				
	$				
Median total income Canada	68,410	69,860	72,240	74,540	76,550
Newfoundland and Labrador	60,290	62,580	67,200	70,900	73,850
Prince Edward Island	62,110	63,610	66,500	69,010	70,270
Nova Scotia	62,550	64,100	66,030	67,910	70,020
New Brunswick	60,670	62,150	63,930	65,910	67,340
Quebec	64,420	65,900	68,170	70,480	72,240
Ontario	69,790	71,540	73,290	74,890	76,510
Manitoba	65,550	66,530	68,710	70,750	72,600
Saskatchewan	70,790	72,650	77,300	80,010	82,990
Alberta	83,560	85,380	89,830	94,460	97,390
British Columbia	66,700	66,970	69,150	71,660	74,150
Yukon	84,640	86,930	91,090	94,460	95,360
Northwest Territories	98,300	101,010	105,560	106,710	109,670
Nunavut	60,160	62,680	65,280	65,530	63,300

1. Census families include couple families, with or without children, and lone-parent families.
Source: Statistics Canada, CANSIM, table 111-0009.
Last modified: 2015-06-26.

And now I'm going to beat a dead horse and include an "Average Salary" poll, which is available online...

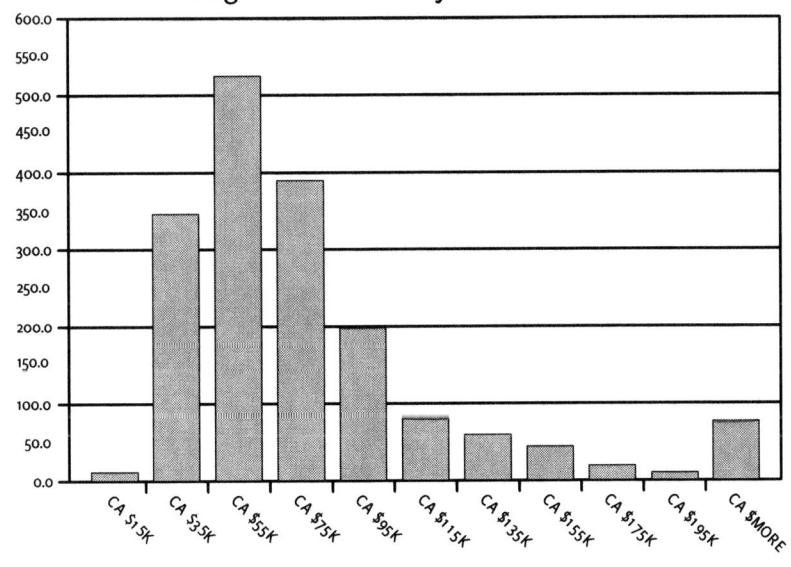

Average Canadian Salary 2016

Frequencies:
Most frequent salary is CA$ 52,697
14.39 % earn at least CA$ 112,481
44.99 % earn at least CA$ 72,997
70.87 % earn at least CA$ 52,697
See more at: http://www.averagesalarysurvey.com/canada #sthash.xvvTGZDM.dpuf

How to Choose a REALTOR® to Sell your Home

Where do you start in choosing a REALTOR® to sell your home? First of all, do not pick a REALTOR® because you think s/he is hot or has celebrity status. This will be the very catalyst that could cause you to greatly dislike your REALTOR® down the road. So back to the question...How do you choose?

You may come to know REALTORS® in many different ways...meeting them at a networking event; referral through someone you know; at your door through solicitation... Whatever the way, you need to decipher what qualities you value in someone who is going to price, showcase, and sell your home. If you don't know off hand, I've summarized the important ones for you.

Experience: The experience REALTORS® should exhibit does not have to be three decades of selling homes. It just means that the experience they have makes them qualified to sell your home. Have they sold homes in your neighbourhood? How many homes have they sold in the past year? What do they specialize in? Do they know the sales trends in the area where your home is located? Do they know how to price your home to result in the best outcome? Do they have life experience that gives them an understanding of your scenario?

Dynamic Marketing: How do they market the homes that they sell? Ask to see photographs and feature sheets. A REALTOR® who has great photographs and feature sheets will be eager to show you. Poor photographs and marketing void of feature sheets are red flags.

Testimonials: People who are pleased with their REALTOR® are usually happy to give a good testimonial. References are ideal as well, but it's not always convenient to contact past clients to ask them to dole out references. When possible, though, these are great.

Communication: Does the REALTOR® communicate in an efficient way? Does s/he return calls quickly and communicate on evenings and weekends? If s/he is part of a team, will s/he still be the primary person looking after the sale of your home? Is s/he up to the times with technology, in order to keep up with other REALTORS®? Does s/he follow up with buyer reps who have seen your home? Does s/he strive for good relations with other REALTORS® or is s/he abrasive, or known as the "tough guy?" Be careful that a REALTOR'S® need to be headstrong does not get in the way of him or her having awareness of the people involved and the delicate details that could have a huge outcome in the sale. What happens if the home doesn't sell? Can your REALTOR® provide informative material to answer ongoing questions you may have?

Honesty: Is your REALTOR® able to tell you the hard things with honesty and sincerity? Will s/he honour your privacy when dealing with the buyers and their REALTOR®?

Refrain from "double ending." This topic has some valid arguments on both sides. Double ending refers to using a REALTOR® who is selling but also representing the buyer who will be making the purchase of your home. This REALTOR® will end up making both sides of the commission; double dipping so to speak, AKA "double ending." I myself will not, under any circumstances, represent both sides. There is no way someone can say with any truth that s/he will not favour one side over another. That being the case, each party deserves personal representation without any outside influence.

How Does Real Estate Commission Work?

Many REALTORS® represent double ending as being advantageous by way of reducing some of the overall commission, but I caution against this practice.

Real estate commission is charged in order to pay the REALTOR® who is representing the seller of the property and the REALTOR® who is representing the buyer of the property. Brokerage fees usually come off each representative's percentage (if applicable).

In Ontario, there is no fixed commission rate or set rate, and it is not legal to fix the rate. That being the case, the typical total "street rate" usually ranges between 5-6%. The REALTOR® who is representing the seller gets about 2.5-3.00% and the REALTOR® who is representing the buyer of the property gets about 2.5-3.00%.

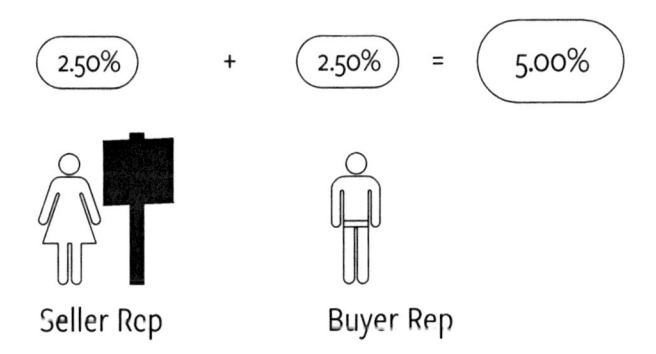

2.50% + 2.50% = 5.00%

Seller Rep   Buyer Rep

Therefore if a $400,000 home has been sold:

$400,000 x 5% = $20,000
$20,000 x 50% = $10,000

The lawyer will collect the HST on the $20,000 separately from the sale proceeds.

Each REALTOR® will have $10,000 sent to his or her brokerage. Fees and tax levies apply thereafter.

A REALTOR® does not always take home the full amount of commission paid by the seller. In fact, in many cases each REALTOR® may only receive about 50-87% (after tax and fees) of the total commission sent to their brokerage. This does not address the REALTOR'S® cost of selling the property, such as advertising, printing costs, staging (if applicable and paid for by the REALTOR®), cash back, and rate discounts. See the example below of how commission can be narrowed through brokerage fees and taxation.

$10,000 commission paid to REALTOR®

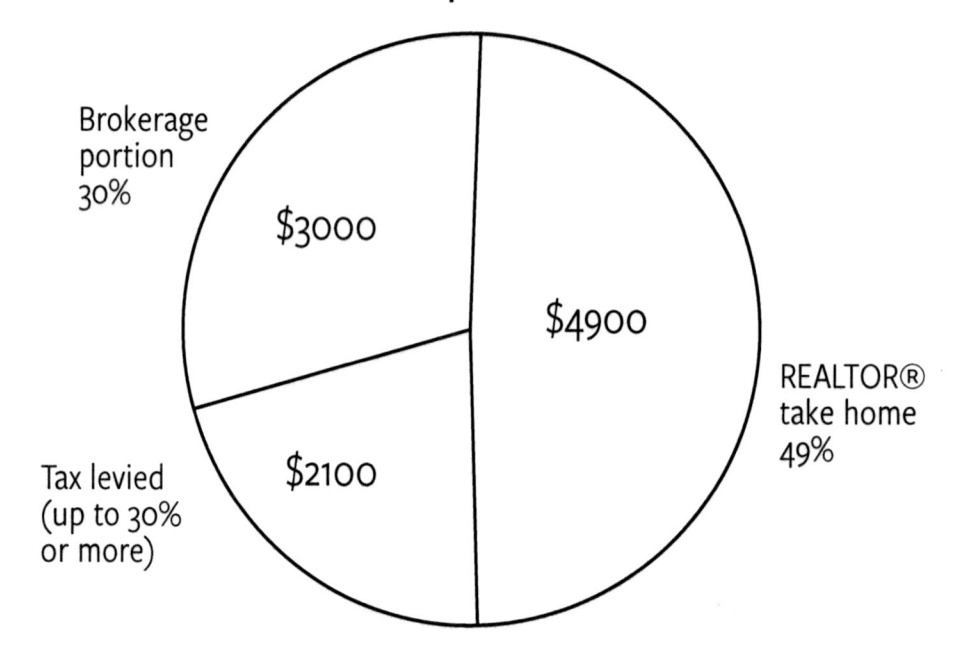

- Brokerage portion 30% — $3000
- $4900
- Tax levied (up to 30% or more) — $2100
- REALTOR® take home 49%

Preparing your Home for Sale

- A kitchen makeover can yield a high return when you're deciding to sell your home. Even small improvements like a new stainless steel microwave and better lighting are highly appealing to home buyers.

- A healthy lawn entices buyers to see the inside of your home. If your lawn is currently patchy and dry, replace it in a single weekend with fresh sod.

- Paint your home in neutral colours. Fresh paint in neutral tones will give your rooms a clean, updated look. Painting is one of the simplest, most cost-effective improvements a homeowner can make.

- Replace carpets and area rugs that have stains or show significant wear. Hardwood, ceramic tile, or laminate all wear well and are popular with home buyers.

- Bathroom updates are ideal. A new vanity, updated lighting, and a ceramic tile floor pay dividends with home buyers. If your toilet is old, it's a good idea to replace it when you install the tile.

- Ask your REALTOR® or your home stager for their expert suggestions on improvements that correspond to the style of your home. Tips such as paint colours, furniture arrangement, and space-saving ideas can sell your home more quickly.

- Visually increase the square footage of your home without demolition. A single, large mirror adds perceived depth. Full-view glass doors as well as de-cluttering lend to the feel of a spacious, more open room.

- Remove all mats and old area rugs. Buyers want to see the floors…not your day to day spillage.

- Window coverings can make or break a room. If a modern window covering is not possible, consider removing window treatments all together. No covering is better than one that dates the room.

- Use good, old-fashioned warm bulbs to light the inside and outside of your home if you don't want to undergo the expense of the new warm toned LED bulbs. Warm lighting is key to comfort. Energy-saving bulbs will save you money, but make your home look like a cafeteria. Non-fluorescent, non-cool white, non-daylight bulbs are best. Incandescent bulbs work well in the photography of your home as well. One off bulb colour can compromise the end result. The basement and garage are the only exceptions for a stylishly lit home.

Staging your home

Staging your home to sell…

…is one of the most misunderstood processes in real estate. The stager's sole role is to make your home appealing to buyers. Stagers often have much difficulty trying to convince the homeowner to remove certain items from the home that would distract or turn off a buyer. I learned this first-hand from one of my toughest clients – my mother!

We were selling my late father's condo, which was located in a town with a less than spectacular job market and a declining home-sale market. A home there was sitting on the market for approximately three to twelve months. We needed to go above and beyond what regular folks were doing to sell their houses in the area, and to de-clutter the entire house. My mother would say to me, "Leave that there, it looks nice."

So…that counter-top-digital-hybrid-clock-weather-meter is going to help sell this place? Oh, and the office chair doubling as a wing-back chair in the living room will do the trick too?

Your buyer does not have the history or background knowledge on why you did what you did to the place. They only know whether they like it or not. A buyer will likely give your home about fifteen minutes to decide if it is on the…

VERY LIKELY TO BUY list

Or on the…

DEFINITELY NOT BUYING list.

There are no maybes, folks. If you have the delusion that someone is going to understand your quirky excuse for the treadmill being in the middle of the living room, you may as well not bother with staging at all – just sell your house for its "as is" state and call it a day.

If you have the means to use a stager to sell your home, you have been granted the gift of an enhanced and justified sale. What I mean by this is that you won't leave dollars on the table when selling your home. Your sale has been given the best potential possible. The home will show its worth, and the price you get for it will be exactly what the market will pay and not less. Use every bit of advice the stager gives you. Sometimes it is not always possible to achieve everything on his/her "to do list" (prior to their coming in to do the final staging), but do try your best.

In this day and age (especially in an urban location), a buyer expects to see a staged home. Sure, another buyer may come along and see the value underneath it all, but it is likely they will lowball your asking price. The cost of hiring a stager is always less than your first price reduction, or (after it has sat on the market for weeks) that final buyer's low offer.

To get back to that example of the sale of my dad's condo...my mother eventually put her stubbornness aside. She let me clear away all the current "décor," as well as any unnecessary items, and I staged it with some new bright and shiny things. We priced the home at what we decided it was worth (not more and not less). It sold in a few days in multiple offers, and we got what we wanted for it. That small town had rarely experienced multiple offers. The buyers did not know what to do and actually thought multiple offers were illegal! It was unheard of. The moral of the story is that a staged home will have an enhanced sale, no matter what town, city, province, demographic, or cultural background is involved.

If you insist on doing the staging yourself and want me to give you one sentence that will encompass everything you need to aim towards to do the job correctly – here it is: Make your home look like a high-end hotel where you stayed (or where you couldn't afford to stay).

What does that look like, you ask?

- All pictures and wall art are without implication. (Use landscapes, abstract paintings, trees, objects, etc.) No pictures of your beautiful self, family, or friends.
- Should be void of trinkets and knick-knacks and feature only medium to large items. To test this, take a wide-framed picture of the room with your cell phone... If you can't tell what the item is – remove it.
- No floor mats in the bathroom or kitchen.
- Kitchen counters clear of gadgets and appliances.
- Neutral wall colours, neutral flooring, minimal furniture.
- Clean – looks like no one lives there
- No expression of religion, race, or creed.
- Temperature always set for visitors' comfort even if vacant for a while.
- Information left out about features of the surrounding areas if located in a resort town.
- Bathrooms free of anything that's been used. (No toothbrushes, toothpaste, open bars of soap or shampoo in tub, etc.)
- Neutral, simple yet sturdy, quality window coverings.
- Light-coloured, neutral bed linens.
- At least two layers of pillows on the master bed (4+ in total) for a full, inviting appearance.

Another thing you must be familiar with when staging your home (whether you hire a stager, or do it yourself) is the demographic of the buyer. The buyer is usually younger than the seller. Yes, you heard me. The buyer is likely younger than you. This can unsettle some people, because you are doing all this work to appeal to someone younger. Your décor may not appeal to someone who is at an earlier stage in life than you are. Their taste may be different. You may not know the latest trends in décor and home fashion. There are two ways to ensure you are staging to target your buyer:

1. Hire a stager.
2. Get a subscription to a home fashion magazine months before you sell, so you can decorate according to today's trends

Stages of Staging

Here is an example which takes the home-buying demographic into consideration.

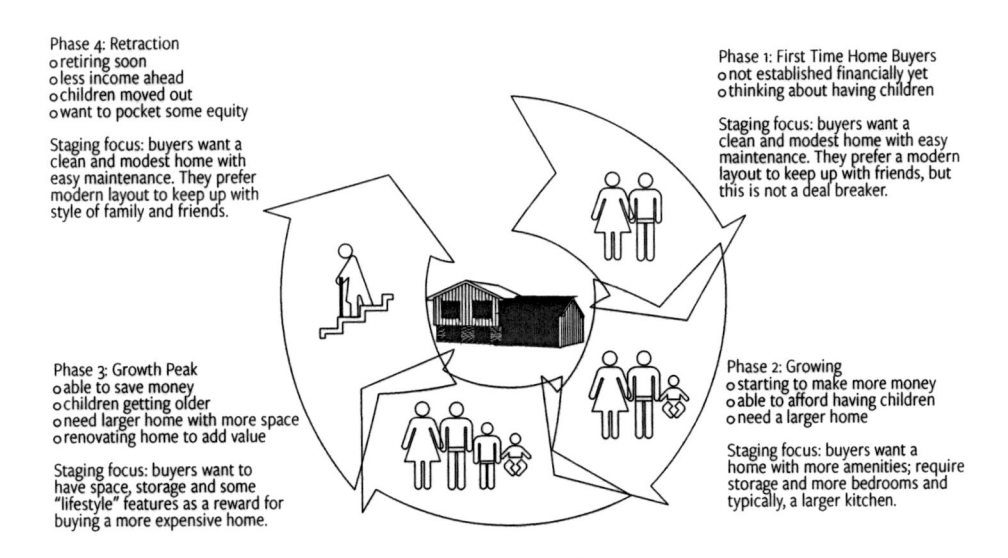

Phase 4: Retraction
o retiring soon
o less income ahead
o children moved out
o want to pocket some equity

Staging focus: buyers want a clean and modest home with easy maintenance. They prefer modern layout to keep up with style of family and friends.

Phase 1: First Time Home Buyers
o not established financially yet
o thinking about having children

Staging focus: buyers want a clean and modest home with easy maintenance. They prefer a modern layout to keep up with friends, but this is not a deal breaker.

Phase 3: Growth Peak
o able to save money
o children getting older
o need larger home with more space
o renovating home to add value

Staging focus: buyers want to have space, storage and some "lifestyle" features as a reward for buying a more expensive home.

Phase 2: Growing
o starting to make more money
o able to afford having children
o need a larger home

Staging focus: buyers want a home with more amenities; require storage and more bedrooms and typically, a larger kitchen.

So as you can see...staging isn't just about making a home look nice. It is a strategic undertaking, which requires knowledge about your demographic and market. You need to understand the best placement of furniture and create flow from one room to another. Colours need to be light and neutral. If you put the extra work in towards the appearance of your home, it will pay off in ease of sale and extra dollars in your pocket!

Take these before-and-after pics as an example of the benefits of staging, (compliments of "Ready to List" staging company). Some show an empty room and how to place furniture accordingly; some show a de-cluttered kitchen, (yes we hate the word de-clutter, but it's a necessary "evil word" in our business), and some show a different furniture layout. Stagers can also bring in furniture to complement the room. Buyers are consumers too and enjoy nice, new, shiny things. If you can't splurge on these things or don't know what to put in your room, hiring a stager is your best and most economical choice. A stager is trained to make your home look its best to prospective buyers. When hiring a professional to sell your home, you shouldn't fall short in making the home look as good as it can.

BEFORE staging

AFTER staging

Christine Denty

BEFORE staging

AFTER staging

*not intended to solicit those under contract

Why Good Photography of your Home is Important

You would think that this would be an obvious no brainer for a home seller... gotta have good pics right? But what exactly constitutes good real estate photography for your home?

Photos should be bright, dynamic, spatially accurate, professional looking, not skewed or stretched, and have some contrast. If your REALTOR'S® pictures fall short of these, you should re-evaluate his or her marketing prowess. Home photography should be top notch and professionally done...bar none.

Here are some examples of good home photography...

Christine Denty

The Girlfriend's Fabulous Guide to Real Estate

You will notice that these photographs pop out from the white page and will be even flashier in colour on the real estate Multiple Listing Service or real estate board where your home will be showcased online. This is important, because when buyers are looking at homes online, these are the ones that will catch their eyes. These photos are basically saying, "Come hither." This is the reaction you want from a buyer. Crappy photos can scare buyers off from even coming to see the home. If this happens, you need to have a serious talking-to with your REALTOR®.

Your Open House

A Few Expectations for Listing your Home

At this point, you might have already done some legwork. You may have begun preparing your home for sale, trimming the hedges, and putting on a fresh coat of paint. However, before your REALTOR® can start showing it off, there are some additional details you should be aware of. First, you should expect your REALTOR® to place a For Sale-sign in the yard. If you are near any major intersections, a sign may go at the intersection as well. You will also be asked to have a lock box hung from your door, so REALTORS® who want to show the home can access it if you are not there.

Hosting Open Houses

As soon as possible after listing your home, your REALTOR® will likely recommend that you hold an open house. The first open house will probably be for local brokers, followed by a public open house for interested buyers and curious neighbours. The brokers' open house is usually held during the week to give local buyer's REALTOR® an opportunity to view the property to see if it will meet the needs of any of their clients. Not long after this, your REALTOR® will likely want to schedule a public open house, which is typically held on a Sunday afternoon. You should plan to be out when there is an open house, so REALTORS® and buyers can tour the home freely.

Keeping Your Home Ready for Showings

Open houses may continue periodically after these initial ones, but the next step is usually showings. You may get little notice before your REALTOR® finds interested buyers who want to see your home, and you should plan to go somewhere else during the showing to give the buyer the freedom to really see your home. You will need to keep your home in tiptop shape during this entire time. Get into some sort of a routine so that you can pick up at a moment's notice and have the home ready for the next showing.

not intended to solicit those under contract

Getting an Offer

The moment you have been waiting for. Your REALTOR® calls you and tells you that you have an offer on your property! The initial reaction is typically excitement. Then reality sets in, when your REALTOR® tells you the offer amount. A first offer is not always at or above your asking price. The excitement fizzles, and the feeling of defeat takes over. Buyers are always trying to get a deal. The amount they pay for your property is reflected in how motivated they are to buy it and their market knowledge on typical pricing for a comparable property. Your REALTOR®, (hopefully) has prepared you for the events surrounding offers and what you should expect as a reasonable offer.

Some of the factors that will affect the offer amounts for your property are:

- current inventory of properties for sale similar to the one you are offering.
- the condition of the property you are offering compared to similar properties
- how long your property has been on the market
- how accurate your price is compared to similar properties for sale
- during what season properties in your region have the highest sales
- whether your neighbourhood is an emerging market or declining one
- visibility to suitable buyers (listed privately or publicly on the Multiple Listing System)
- communication skills, likeability and product knowledge of your REALTOR® in his/her interactions with other REALTORS®.
- integrity of photos and marketing of the property

Elements of a Purchase and Sale Agreement (the document that transacts the buying and selling of a property into a binding contract):

An accepted offer is a legally binding contract between a buyer (the offerer) and a seller (offeree). Sometimes it can be reversed where the seller becomes the offerer by proposing a price to the buyer, who would then be the offeree. The other elements traditionally required for a legally binding contract are:

The Girlfriend's Fabulous Guide to Real Estate

- consideration (typically in a real estate transaction there is a deposit amount)
- an intention to create legal relations (the transaction makes sense and is advantageous to both parties)

Following is a breakdown of the OREA "Agreement of Purchase and Sale." It is recommended that everyone seek and obtain professional advice to gain a complete and accurate understanding of any legal form, and not to rely on the explanations contained herein.

OREA Ontario Real Estate Association

Agreement of Purchase and Sale

Form 100 for use in the Province of Ontario

This Agreement of Purchase and Sale dated this 1 day of April 20 15.

BUYER, John Doe .... (Full legal names of all Buyers), agrees to purchase from

SELLER, Jane Dee .... (Full legal names of all Sellers), the following

REAL PROPERTY:

Address 5 Smith Street

fronting on the South side of Smith Street

in the Municipality of Ajax

and having a frontage of 50 feet more or less by a depth of 104.9 feet more or less

and legally described as Lot 151 Plan M102

.... (legal description of land including easements not described elsewhere) (the "property").

PURCHASE PRICE: Dollars (CDN$) 300,000.00

Three Hundred Thousand .... Dollars

DEPOSIT: Buyer submits Upon acceptance
(Herewith/Upon Acceptance/as otherwise described in this Agreement)

Ten Thousand .... Dollars (CDN$) 10,000.00

by negotiable cheque payable to MINFEE REAL ESTATE INC. .... "Deposit Holder"
to be held in trust pending completion or other termination of this Agreement and to be credited toward the Purchase Price on completion. For the purposes of this Agreement, "Upon Acceptance" shall mean that the Buyer is required to deliver the deposit to the Deposit Holder within 24 hours of the acceptance of this Agreement. The parties to this Agreement hereby acknowledge that, unless otherwise provided for in this Agreement, the Deposit Holder shall place the deposit in trust in the Deposit Holder's non-interest bearing Real Estate Trust Account and no interest shall be earned, received or paid on the deposit.

Buyer agrees to pay the balance as more particularly set out in Schedule A attached.

SCHEDULE(S) A .... attached hereto form(s) part of this Agreement.

1. **IRREVOCABILITY:** This offer shall be irrevocable by Buyer (Seller/Buyer) until 4:00 p.m. on the 1 day of April 20 15, after which time, if not accepted, this offer shall be null and void and the deposit shall be returned to the Buyer in full without interest.

2. **COMPLETION DATE:** This Agreement shall be completed by no later than 6:00 p.m. on the 30 day of June, 20 15. Upon completion, vacant possession of the property shall be given to the Buyer unless otherwise provided for in this Agreement.

INITIALS OF BUYER(S): ( )   **INITIALS OF SELLER(S):** ( )

© 2015, Ontario Real Estate Association ("OREA"). All rights reserved. This form was developed by OREA for the use and reproduction of its members and licensees only. Any other use or reproduction is prohibited except with prior written consent of OREA. Do not alter when printing or reproducing the standard pre-set portion. **Form 100** Revised 2015 **Page 1 of 6**

not intended to solicit those under contract

Buyer

The person, persons, or entity agreeing to buy the property.

Seller

The person, persons or entity agreeing to sell the property.

Real Property

The subset of land with or without buildings and improvements. In this section the address and legal description of the property are described.

Purchase Price

This is the agreed-upon price to purchase the property. Often this can be scratched out and rewritten several times before an agreement on price is made. This is typically one of the areas of most focus when a seller receives an offer.

Deposit

This is the monetary amount the buyer is willing to put down for consideration to bind the contract (if accepted). Usually this entire amount goes towards the buyer's down payment, in addition to other deposits required to purchase the property. If the buyer decides to provide this deposit "Upon Acceptance," this deposit (via certified cheque or draft)is required to be delivered to the selling brokerage within 24 hours of the offer being accepted. Failing this, the agreement could be null and void, hence no sale would occur. The balance of the purchase price is addressed in the Schedule "A" of the agreement. Typically worded: "The Buyer agrees to pay the balance of the purchase price, subject to adjustments, to the Seller on completion date of this transaction, with funds drawn on a lawyer's trust account in the form of a bank draft, certified cheque or wire transfer using the Large Value Transfer System."

Schedules

This document or documents are attached to the Agreement of Purchase and Sale in the form of : "Schedule A, B, C..." etc. These documents outline other elements agreed upon by the buyer and seller, which make up the entire agreement. These elements are termed as standard or custom clauses. See example for page 6 of the Agreement of Purchase and Sale.

Irrevocability

This outlines who is extending the offer and how long they are allowing the buyer or seller to accept, sign it back with changes, or decline the offer. Irrevocable basically means that the offeror cannot withdraw this offer until the date and time set out in this section of the Agreement of Purchase and Sale. They must permit the full extent of time allotted for the offeror to respond.

Completion Date

This is the closing date for the sale. Keys and enjoyment of the property should be made available by this date. All terms of the agreement need to be met by this date at the latest.

3. **NOTICES:** The Seller hereby appoints the Listing Brokerage as agent for the Seller for the purpose of giving and receiving notices pursuant to this Agreement. Where a Brokerage (Buyer's Brokerage) has entered into a representation agreement with the Buyer, the Buyer hereby appoints the Buyer's Brokerage as agent for the purpose of giving and receiving notices pursuant to this Agreement. **Where a Brokerage represents both the Seller and the Buyer (multiple representation), the Brokerage shall not be appointed or authorized to be agent for either the Buyer or the Seller for the purpose of giving and receiving notices.** Any notice relating hereto or provided for herein shall be in writing. In addition to any provision contained herein and in any Schedule hereto, this offer, any counter-offer, notice of acceptance thereof or any notice to be given or received pursuant to this Agreement or any Schedule hereto (any of them, "Document") shall be deemed given and received when delivered personally or hand delivered to the Address for Service provided in the Acknowledgement below, or where a facsimile number or email address is provided herein, when transmitted electronically to that facsimile number or email address, respectively, in which case, the signature(s) of the party (parties) shall be deemed to be original.

FAX No.: .... FAX No.: ....905-665-3167................
(For delivery of Documents to Seller)   (For delivery of Documents to Buyer)

Email Address: .... Email Address: denty.christine@gmail.com
(For delivery of Documents to Seller)   (For delivery of Documents to Buyer)

4. **CHATTELS INCLUDED:**
   2 Fridges, 2 Stoves, 1 B/I Dishwasher, Washer, Dryer, All ELF's, All Window Coverings, Shed in Backyard

   Unless otherwise stated in this Agreement or any Schedule hereto, Seller agrees to convey all fixtures and chattels included in the Purchase Price free from all liens, encumbrances or claims affecting the said fixtures and chattels.

5. **FIXTURES EXCLUDED:**

6. **RENTAL ITEMS (Including Lease, Lease to Own):** The following equipment is rented and **not** included in the Purchase Price. The Buyer agrees to assume the rental contract(s), if assumable:
   Hot Water Tank (if rental)

   The Buyer agrees to co-operate and execute such documentation as may be required to facilitate such assumption.

7. **HST:** If the sale of the property (Real Property as described above) is subject to Harmonized Sales Tax (HST), then such tax shall be ..included in.................................. the Purchase Price. If the sale of the property is not subject to HST, Seller agrees to certify on or before closing, that the sale of the property is not subject to HST. Any HST on chattels, if applicable, is not included in the Purchase Price.

Notices

This is the appointment of the brokerages to act as agents for the purpose of giving and receiving notices pursuant to the agreement. Your REALTOR'S® contact info would likely be listed here as well as the other party's REALTOR'S® contact info. It is important that the contact information is up to date as all communication will take place will use it.

Chattels Included

These are all the appliances, fixtures and items that are to remain in the property as part of the interest in the sale. These typically are: Fridge, Stove, Washer, Dryer, Built-in Dishwasher, Electrical Light Fixtures, Window Coverings, Back yard Shed, to name a few. Chattels do not always mean something affixed to the property. At times, people negotiate riding mowers, water-softening systems, furniture, TVs affixed to the walls, closet storage systems, etc. It is not typical to have a long list of extra chattels. To do so may turn off the seller and complicate the sale.

Fixtures Excluded

This outlines any items that are reasonably assumed as included, but are elected to be excluded. Often this could be a new washer and dryer that the sellers just bought which they would like to take with them; custom built cabinetry; water-softening system; mirrors; a designer dining room light fixture, etc.

Rental Items

This lists the items that are not owned in the home, for which there is a lease or rental contract in place. The buyer is deemed to assume the current terms of the current contract unless otherwise stated. The most common item listed is the hot water tank (if rental).

HST

HST is typically included in the purchase price of a home in Canada. In a "new build" (you purchase the home before it is built) it can be transacted and charged on top of the purchase price, but that's not likely with the resale of a property.

8. **TITLE SEARCH:** Buyer shall be allowed until 6:00 p.m. on the 19 day of June, 20 15, (Requisition Date) to examine the title to the property at Buyer's own expense and until the earlier of: (i) thirty days from the later of the Requisition Date or the date on which the conditions in this Agreement are fulfilled or otherwise waived or; (ii) five days prior to completion, to satisfy Buyer that there are no outstanding work orders or deficiency notices affecting the property, and that its present use (single family residential) may be lawfully continued and that the principal building may be insured against risk of fire. Seller hereby consents to the municipality or other governmental agencies releasing to Buyer details of all outstanding work orders and deficiency notices affecting the property, and Seller agrees to execute and deliver such further authorizations in this regard as Buyer may reasonably require.

9. **FUTURE USE:** Seller and Buyer agree that there is no representation or warranty of any kind that the future intended use of the property by Buyer is or will be lawful except as may be specifically provided for in this Agreement.

10. **TITLE:** Provided that the title to the property is good and free from all registered restrictions, charges, liens, and encumbrances except as otherwise specifically provided in this Agreement and save and except for (a) any registered restrictions or covenants that run with the land providing that such are complied with; (b) any registered municipal agreements and registered agreements with publicly regulated utilities providing such have been complied with, or security has been posted to ensure compliance and completion, as evidenced by a letter from the relevant municipality or regulated utility; (c) any minor easements for the supply of domestic utility or telephone services to the property or adjacent properties; and (d) any easements for drainage, storm or sanitary sewers, public utility lines, telephone lines, cable television lines or other services which do not materially affect the use of the property. If within the specified times referred to in paragraph 8 any valid objection to title or to any outstanding work order or deficiency notice, or to the fact the said present use may not lawfully be continued, or that the principal building may not be insured against risk of fire is made in writing to Seller and which Seller is unable or unwilling to remove, remedy or satisfy or obtain insurance save and except against risk of fire (Title Insurance) in favour of the Buyer and any mortgagee, (with all related costs at the expense of the Seller), and which Buyer will not waive, this Agreement notwithstanding any intermediate acts or negotiations in respect of such objections, shall be at an end and all monies paid shall be returned without interest or deduction and Seller, Listing Brokerage and Co-operating Brokerage shall not be liable for any costs or damages. Save as to any valid objection so made by such day and except for any objection going to the root of the title, Buyer shall be conclusively deemed to have accepted Seller's title to the property.

11. **CLOSING ARRANGEMENTS:** Where each of the Seller and Buyer retain a lawyer to complete the Agreement of Purchase and Sale of the property, and where the transaction will be completed by electronic registration pursuant to Part III of the Land Registration Reform Act, R.S.O. 1990, Chapter L4 and the Electronic Registration Act, S.O. 1991, Chapter 44, and any amendments thereto, the Seller and Buyer acknowledge and agree that the exchange of closing funds, non-registrable documents and other items (the "Requisite Deliveries") and the release thereof to the Seller and Buyer will (a) not occur at the same time as the registration of the transfer/deed (and any other documents intended to be registered in connection with the completion of this transaction) and (b) be subject to conditions whereby the lawyer(s) receiving any of the Requisite Deliveries will be required to hold same in trust and not release same except in accordance with the terms of a document registration agreement between the said lawyers. The Seller and Buyer irrevocably instruct the said lawyers to be bound by the document registration agreement which is recommended from time to time by the Law Society of Upper Canada. Unless otherwise agreed to by the lawyers, such exchange of the Requisite Deliveries will occur in the applicable Land Titles Office or such other location agreeable to both lawyers.

12. **DOCUMENTS AND DISCHARGE:** Buyer shall not call for the production of any title deed, abstract, survey or other evidence of title to the property except such as are in the possession or control of Seller. If requested by Buyer, Seller will deliver any sketch or survey of the property within Seller's control to Buyer as soon as possible and prior to the Requisition Date. If a discharge of any Charge/Mortgage held by a corporation incorporated pursuant to the Trust And Loan Companies Act (Canada), Chartered Bank, Trust Company, Credit Union, Caisse Populaire or Insurance Company and which is not to be assumed by Buyer on completion, is not available in registrable form on completion, Buyer agrees to accept Seller's lawyer's personal undertaking to obtain, out of the closing funds, a discharge in registrable form and to register same, or cause same to be registered, on title within a reasonable period of time after completion, provided that on or before completion Seller shall provide to Buyer a mortgage statement prepared by the mortgagee setting out the balance required to obtain the discharge, and, where a real-time electronic cleared funds transfer system is not being used, a direction executed by Seller directing payment to the mortgagee of the amount required to obtain the discharge out of the balance due on completion.

13. **INSPECTION:** Buyer acknowledges having had the opportunity to inspect the property and understands that upon acceptance of this offer there shall be a binding agreement of purchase and sale between Buyer and Seller. **The Buyer acknowledges having the opportunity to include a requirement for a property inspection report in this Agreement and agrees that except as may be specifically provided for in this Agreement, the Buyer will not be obtaining a property inspection or property inspection report regarding the property.**

INITIALS OF BUYER(S): INITIALS OF SELLER(S):

Title Search

This section provides the times for the buyer's lawyer to do the necessary searches on the property. These will likely include matters such as checking the title to ensure that the Buyer is going to obtain good title and that there is no outstanding work orders. It also confirms the present use of the property and its lawful continuance of such.

Future Use

This declares an agreement between the buyer and seller that the future use as something else cannot be assured or guaranteed. For example, a buyer may be purchasing a property in order to turn it into a triplex. The seller cannot guarantee the buyer will be able to get lawful zoning and permission to do so.

Title

This section provides that the buyer is entitled to clean title but must accept the title subject to any easements for the supply of telephone services, electricity, gas, sewers, water, television cable facilities and other related services. Also the buyer has to accept the title subject to any restrictive covenants as long as they are complied with. Finally if there are any municipal agreements, zoning bylaws or utility or service contracts, the buyer would be assuming them. This may be of special concern though for a Power of Sale or a Foreclosure as Title Insurance may only provide for risk of fire but not for any outstanding liens or encumbrances (without a lengthy process to address the issues). If the liens or claims prove to be too much you could be asked to remedy (when it comes time for you to sell) and it could be very costly.

Closing Arrangements

This section sets out how the lawyers will set out the exchange of title between seller and buyer as well as the order of the procedure. Lawyers can exercise the electronic method or the manual method. Both are addressed here.

Documents and Discharge

This section states that the buyer cannot insist on the seller providing a survey, abstract or deed; only what the seller is in possession of can be requested but not demanded. This also sets out how the mortgage discharge is to take place (between seller and their lawyer). The buyer cannot (nor their lawyer) make demands to have the mortgage paid off before closing but is to assume it is completed by closing.

Inspection

This section addresses matters about a property inspection. It outlines that it is not the seller's obligation to provide you with a property inspection. Conversely, if agreed by the seller and the buyer, an inspection may be performed. If it is waived you do not have the right to demand one from the seller.

Insurance

This section addresses that the seller needs to maintain insurance until closing. If the property burns down, the buyer can either continue the deal or use the proceeds to rebuild or back out of the deal. It also states that the buyer cannot assume the seller's insurance. They need to obtain their own separate insurance policy.

Planning Act

This section states that the Agreement is subject to compliance with the Planning Act. This statute governs things like severance (splitting a property into two, to build or sell).

Document Preparation

This section sets out that the seller pays for their own discharge and the buyer pays to have their own mortgage provided to them. Residency: This section addresses that the seller needs to notify the buyer if they are a non-resident. In doing so they must either provide the buyer with enough extra funds to pay the Minister of National Revenue so that the buyer does not have any liability or pay the funds directly to cover the liability.

Adjustments

This section states that certain charges applicable to the property such as property taxes, rents or utilities will be adjusted on the completion day. The buyer will assume responsibility beginning on the day of the completion of the sale.

Property Assessment

This section states that property taxes may go up during or after the sale and the seller (or salespeople) would not liable if this happens.

Time Limits

This section states that the buyer and seller (if agreeable) can extend time limits for different matters in the agreement.

Tender

This section states how monies may be paid at closing. Assuming they are paid in full, the sale must be completed.

Family Law Act

This section sets out that unless a document is provided to declare such, no spousal consent is necessary. This comes into the agreement if for example only a husband is on title for the matrimonial home and he wishes to sell the home. He needs his spouse to agree to the sale before it can take place.

UFFI

The Seller warrants that while owning the property they have not used insulation containing urea formaldehyde. Also, the Seller is not aware of that kind of insulation ever having been used on or within the property.

Legal, Accounting, and Environmental Advice

This section notes the release of responsibility of the brokerages regarding tax, legal and environmental advice. A professional in those particular fields should always be consulted regarding these issues.

Consumer Reports

During the financing phase of the purchase the buyer will likely have a Consumer Report ordered to determine the credit worthiness of the buyer for the financing.

Agreement in Writing

This section states that this Agreement shall be taken as final EXCEPT if any agreed upon provisions take place thereafter. This also states that there are no other agreements in existence other than this document.

Time and Date

This notes that whatever time zone the property is located shall be considered as the referenced time for the agreement and completion dates.

14. **INSURANCE:** All buildings on the property and all other things being purchased shall be and remain until completion at the risk of Seller. Pending completion, Seller shall hold all insurance policies, if any, and the proceeds thereof in trust for the parties as their interests may appear and in the event of substantial damage, Buyer may either terminate this Agreement and have all monies paid returned without interest or deduction or else take the proceeds of any insurance and complete the purchase. No insurance shall be transferred on completion. If Seller is taking back a Charge/Mortgage, or Buyer is assuming a Charge/Mortgage, Buyer shall supply Seller with reasonable evidence of adequate insurance to protect Seller's or other mortgagee's interest on completion.

15. **PLANNING ACT:** This Agreement shall be effective to create an interest in the property only if Seller complies with the subdivision control provisions of the Planning Act by completion and Seller covenants to proceed diligently at Seller's expense to obtain any necessary consent by completion.

16. **DOCUMENT PREPARATION:** The Transfer/Deed shall, save for the Land Transfer Tax Affidavit, be prepared in registrable form at the expense of Seller, and any Charge/Mortgage to be given back by the Buyer to Seller at the expense of the Buyer. If requested by Buyer, Seller covenants that the Transfer/Deed to be delivered on completion shall contain the statements contemplated by Section 50(22) of the Planning Act, R.S.O.1990.

17. **RESIDENCY:** (a) Subject to (b) below, the Seller represents and warrants that the Seller is not and on completion will not be a non-resident under the non-residency provisions of the Income Tax Act which representation and warranty shall survive and not merge upon the completion of this transaction and the Seller shall deliver to the Buyer a statutory declaration that Seller is not then a non-resident of Canada;
(b) provided that if the Seller is a non-resident under the non-residency provisions of the Income Tax Act, the Buyer shall be credited towards the Purchase Price with the amount, if any, necessary for Buyer to pay to the Minister of National Revenue to satisfy Buyer's liability in respect of tax payable by Seller under the non-residency provisions of the Income Tax Act by reason of this sale. Buyer shall not claim such credit if Seller delivers on completion the prescribed certificate.

18. **ADJUSTMENTS:** Any rents, mortgage interest, realty taxes including local improvement rates and unmetered public or private utility charges and unmetered cost of fuel, as applicable, shall be apportioned and allowed to the day of completion, the day of completion itself to be apportioned to Buyer.

19. **PROPERTY ASSESSMENT:** The Buyer and Seller hereby acknowledge that the Province of Ontario has implemented current value assessment and properties may be re-assessed on an annual basis. The Buyer and Seller agree that no claim will be made against the Buyer or Seller, or any Brokerage, Broker or Salesperson, for any changes in property tax as a result of a re-assessment of the property, save and except any property taxes that accrued prior to the completion of this transaction.

20. **TIME LIMITS:** Time shall in all respects be of the essence hereof provided that the time for doing or completing of any matter provided for herein may be extended or abridged by an agreement in writing signed by Seller and Buyer or by their respective lawyers who may be specifically authorized in that regard.

21. **TENDER:** Any tender of documents or money hereunder may be made upon Seller or Buyer or their respective lawyers on the day set for completion. Money shall be tendered with funds drawn on a lawyer's trust account in the form of a bank draft, certified cheque or wire transfer using the Large Value Transfer System.

22. **FAMILY LAW ACT:** Seller warrants that spousal consent is not necessary to this transaction under the provisions of the Family Law Act, R.S.O.1990 unless Seller's spouse has executed the consent hereinafter provided.

23. **UFFI:** Seller represents and warrants to Buyer that during the time Seller has owned the property, Seller has not caused any building on the property to be insulated with insulation containing ureaformaldehyde, and that to the best of Seller's knowledge no building on the property contains or has ever contained insulation that contains ureaformaldehyde. This warranty shall survive and not merge on the completion of this transaction, and if the building is part of a multiple unit building, this warranty shall only apply to that part of the building which is the subject of this transaction.

24. **LEGAL, ACCOUNTING AND ENVIRONMENTAL ADVICE:** The parties acknowledge that any information provided by the brokerage is not legal, tax or environmental advice.

25. **CONSUMER REPORTS: The Buyer is hereby notified that a consumer report containing credit and/or personal information may be referred to in connection with this transaction.**

26. **AGREEMENT IN WRITING:** If there is conflict or discrepancy between any provision added to this Agreement (including any Schedule attached hereto) and any provision in the standard pre-set portion hereof, the added provision shall supersede the standard pre-set provision to the extent of such conflict or discrepancy. This Agreement including any Schedule attached hereto, shall constitute the entire Agreement between Buyer and Seller. There is no representation, warranty, collateral agreement or condition, which affects this Agreement other than as expressed herein. For the purposes of this Agreement, Seller means vendor and Buyer means purchaser. This Agreement shall be read with all changes of gender or number required by the context.

27. **TIME AND DATE:** Any reference to a time and date in this Agreement shall mean the time and date where the property is located.

INITIALS OF BUYER(S):   INITIALS OF SELLER(S):

Insurance

This section addresses that the seller needs to maintain insurance until closing. If the property burns down, the buyer can either continue the deal and/or use the proceeds to rebuild or back out of the deal. It also states that the buyer cannot assume the seller's insurance. They need to obtain their own separate insurance policy.

Planning Act

This section states that the Agreement is subject to compliance with the Planning Act. This statute governs things like severance (splitting a property into two, to build or sell).

Document Preparation

This section sets out that the seller pays for their own discharge and the buyer pays to have their own mortgage provided to them.

Residency

This section addresses that the seller needs to notify the buyer if they are a non-resident. In doing so they must either provide the buyer with enough extra funds to pay the Minister of National Revenue so that the buyer does not have any liability or pay the funds directly to cover the liability.

Adjustments

This section states that certain charges applicable to the property such as property taxes, rents or utilities will be adjusted on the completion day. The buyer will assume responsibility beginning on the day of the completion of the sale.

Property Assessment

This section states that property taxes may go up during or after the sale and the seller (or salespeople) would not liable if this happens.

Time Limits

This section states that the buyer and seller (if agreeable) can extend time limits for different matters in the agreement.

Tender

This section states how monies may be paid at closing. Assuming they are paid in full, the sale must be completed.

Family Law Act

Explained on previous page.

UFFI

The Seller warrants that while owning the property they have not used insulation containing urea formaldehyde. Also, the Seller is not aware of that kind of insulation ever having been used on or within the property.

Legal, Accounting, and Environmental Advice

This section notes the release of responsibility of the brokerages regarding tax, legal and environmental advice. A professional in those particular fields should always be consulted regarding these issues.

Consumer Reports

During the financing phase of the purchase the buyer will likely have a Consumer Report ordered to determine the credit worthiness of the buyer for the financing.

Agreement in Writing

This section states that this Agreement shall be taken as final EXCEPT if any agreed upon provisions take place thereafter. This also states that there are no other agreements in existence other than this document.

Time and Date

This notes that whatever time zone the property is located shall be considered as the referenced time for the agreement and completion dates.

Successors and Assigns

This declares that if the buyer passes away, his or her heirs and/or executors are bound by this agreement.

Spousal Consent

This section is signed by a spouse to acknowledge and permit the sale of the property. It also states that the spouse who signs this acknowledges that they have received (or are privy to) copies of all the sale documents for the transaction taking place.

Confirmation of Acceptance

In this section the buyer or seller make the last terms offered to them a final agreement. Information no Brokerages: Self-explanatory.

Acknowledgement

This section is to be signed only when the buyer and seller have received a copy of the completed Purchase and Sale Agreement. It should be completed on the spot with address and lawyer information so that the brokerages know where to forward documents if need be and which lawyers the buyer and seller will be using.

OREA Ontario Real Estate Association

Schedule A
Agreement of Purchase and Sale

Form 100 for use in the Province of Ontario

This Schedule is attached to and forms part of the Agreement of Purchase and Sale between:

BUYER, John Doe, and

SELLER, Jane Dee

for the purchase and sale of 5 Smith Street

Ajax L1S 2Z9 dated the 1 day of April, 2015.

Buyer agrees to pay the balance as follows:

The Buyer agrees to pay the balance of the purchase price, subject to adjustments, to the Seller on completion of this transaction, with funds drawn on a lawyer's trust account in the form of a bank draft, certified cheque or wire transfer using the Large Value Transfer System.

This Offer is conditional upon the Buyer arranging, at the Buyer's own expense, a new first Charge/Mortgage satisfactory to the Buyer in the Buyer's sole and absolute discretion. Unless the Buyer gives notice in writing delivered to the Seller personally or in accordance with any other provisions for the delivery of notice in this Agreement of Purchase and Sale or any Schedule thereto not later than 6:00 p.m. on January 23, 2015, that this condition is fulfilled, this Offer shall be null and void and the deposit shall be returned to the Buyer in full without deduction. This condition is included for the benefit of the Buyer and may be waived at the Buyer's sole option by notice in writing to the Seller as aforesaid within the time period stated herein.

This offer is conditional on the Buyer arranging insurance for the property satisfactory to the Buyer in the Buyer's sole and absolute discretion. Unless the Buyer gives notice in writing delivered to the Seller personally or in accordance with any other provisions for the delivery of notice in this Agreement of Purchase and Sale or any Schedule thereto not later than 6:00 p.m. on January 23, 2015, that this condition is fulfilled, this offer shall be null and void and the deposit shall be returned to the Buyer in full without deduction. The Seller agrees to co-operate in providing access to the property, if necessary, for any inspection of the property required for the fulfillment of this condition. This condition is included for the benefit of the Buyer and may be waived at the Buyer's sole option by notice in writing to the Seller as aforesaid within the time period stated herein.

This Offer is conditional upon the inspection of the subject property by a home inspector at the Buyer's own expense, and the obtaining of a report satisfactory to the Buyer in the Buyer's sole and absolute discretion. Unless the Buyer gives notice in writing delivered to the Seller personally or in accordance with any other provisions for the delivery of notice in this Agreement of Purchase and Sale or any Schedule thereto not later than 6:00 p.m. on January 23, 2015, that this condition is fulfilled, this Offer shall be null and void and the deposit shall be returned to the Buyer in full without deduction. The Seller agrees to co-operate in providing access to the property for the purpose of this inspection. This condition is included for the benefit of the Buyer and may be waived at the Buyer's sole option by notice in writing to the Seller as aforesaid within the time period stated herein.

The Seller represents and warrants that the chattels and fixtures as included in this Agreement of Purchase and Sale will be in good working order and free from all liens and encumbrances on completion. The Parties agree that this representation and warranty shall survive and not merge on completion of this transaction, but apply only to the state of the property at completion of this transaction.

The Seller Agrees to provide access to the Buyer for 2 revisits subject to 24 hours notice prior to completion date.

This form must be initialed by all parties to the Agreement of Purchase and Sale.

INITIALS OF BUYER(S): **INITIALS OF SELLER(S):**

Schedules

This document or documents are attached to the Agreement of Purchase and Sale in the form of : "Schedule A, B, C..." etc. These documents outline other elements agreed upon by the buyer and seller which make up the entire agreement. These elements are termed as standard or custom clauses. Common clauses found on a Schedule are:

"The Buyer agrees to pay the balance of the purchase price, subject to adjustments, to the Seller on completion of this transaction, with funds drawn on a lawyer's trust account in the form of a bank draft, certified cheque or wire transfer using the Large Value Transfer System."

"This Offer is conditional upon the Buyer arranging, at the Buyer's own expense, a new first or second Charge/Mortgage satisfactory to the Buyer in the Buyer's sole and absolute discretion. Unless the Buyer gives notice in writing delivered to the Seller personally or in accordance with any other provisions for the delivery of notice in this Agreement of Purchase and Sale or any Schedule thereto not later than 6:00 p.m. on April 21, 2015, that this condition is fulfilled, this Offer shall be null and void and the deposit shall be returned to the Buyer in full without deduction. This condition is included for the benefit of the Buyer and may be waived at the Buyer's sole option by notice in writing to the Seller as aforesaid within the time period stated herein."

"This Offer is conditional upon the inspection of the subject property by a home inspector at the Buyer's own expense, and the obtaining of a report satisfactory to the Buyer in the Buyer's sole and absolute discretion. Unless the Buyer gives notice in writing delivered to the Seller personally or in accordance with any other provisions for the delivery of notice in this Agreement of Purchase and Sale or any Schedule thereto not later than 6:00 p.m. on April 21, 2015, that this condition is fulfilled, this Offer shall be null and void and the deposit shall be returned to the Buyer in full without deduction. The Seller agrees to co-operate in providing access to the property for the purpose of this inspection. This condition is included for the benefit of the Buyer and may be waived at the Buyer's sole option by notice in writing to the Seller as aforesaid within the time period stated herein."

"This offer is conditional on the Buyer arranging insurance for the property satisfactory to the Buyer in the Buyer's sole and absolute discretion. Unless the Buyer gives notice in writing delivered to the Seller personally or in accordance with any other provisions for the delivery of notice in this Agreement of Purchase and Sale or any Schedule thereto not later than 6:00 p.m. on April 8, 2015, that this condition is fulfilled, this offer shall be null and void and the deposit shall be returned to the Buyer in full without deduction. The Seller agrees to co-operate in providing access to the property, if necessary, for any inspection of the property required for the fulfillment of this condition. This condition is included for the benefit of the Buyer and may be waived at the Buyer's sole option by notice in writing to the Seller as aforesaid within the time period stated herein." (This is typically only included for older properties that may have wiring or structural issues).

"The Seller represents and warrants that the chattels and fixtures as included in this Agreement of Purchase and Sale will be in good working order and free from all liens and encumbrances on completion. The Parties agree that this representation and warranty shall survive and not merge on completion of this transaction, but apply only to the state of the property at completion of this transaction."

"The Seller represents and warrants that during the time the Seller has owned the property, the use of the property and the buildings and structures thereon has not been for the growth or manufacture of any illegal substances, and that to the best of the Seller's knowledge and belief, the use of the property and the buildings and structures thereon has never been for the growth or manufacture of illegal substances. This warranty shall survive and not merge on the completion of this transaction."

For Condos only: "This offer is conditional upon the Buyer's lawyer reviewing the Status Certificate and Attachments and finding the Status Certificate and Attachments satisfactory in the Buyer's Lawyer's sole and absolute discretion. The Seller agrees to request at the Seller's expense, the Status Certificate and attachments within 5 days after acceptance of this Offer. Unless the buyer gives notice in writing to the Seller personally or in accordance with any other provisions for the delivery of notice in this Agreement of Purchase and Sale or any Schedule thereto not later than 5 p.m. on the fifth day (excluding Saturdays, Sundays and Statutory Holidays) following receipt by the buyer of the Status Certificate and attachments, that this condition is fulfilled, this Offer shall be null and void and the deposit shall be returned to the Buyer in full without deduction. This condition is included for the benefit of the Buyer and may be waived at the Buyer's sole option by notice in writing to the Seller as aforesaid within the time period stated herein."

There are potentially hundreds of different clauses that can be written into an agreement. Clauses can directly affect the success of a transaction or change its terms dramatically. Buyers and Sellers should exercise extreme caution when including and waiving clauses. The absence of certain clauses puts the buyer (and sometimes the seller) at risk. On the other hand too many clauses will put off a seller and likely result in a buyer's offer getting turned down. Lawyers pay much attention to how clauses are written. They track fulfillments of clauses and take the terms very seriously. A clause should not be included unless it is realistic, comprehensive, and written in legal terms.

Seller's Closing Costs

So you've sold your house, that's fantastic! But I'm going to burst your bubble (same way I did in the Buyer's Closing Cost chapter). The price you received for the sale of your home is not final. There are a few costs associated with selling your home. Here are some of them:

Status Certificate

(For condo sales only) This certificate is requested by the buyer upon an accepted offer. It outlines the financial, structural, and communal health of the Condo Corporation and building. The cost is about $200. The buyer's lawyer will review the information in the certificate and counsel the buyer on whether or not to proceed.

Survey

If a survey is available, the cost to acquire it is minimal. If one is not available and the buyer insists on it, or there is a dispute regarding property lines or easements, you may have to have a new survey produced. This could cost upwards of $1000.

Legal Fees

Lawyers vary in pricing, and you might expect to pay $400-$800, not including disbursements. It is not a bad thing to take your REALTOR'S® opinion on who to use if you don't have one in mind. A busy REALTOR® works with lawyers quite a bit. Also if you have a friend, co-worker or family member who has had a good experience this is also a good place to start. It is a good idea to look them up on the Better Business Bureau as well to see if there have been any real issues in the past. http://www.bbb.org/

Staging

Your stager will require funds upfront or immediately after the staging has taken place. The cost of this may vary from stager to stager – $500-$10000.

REALTOR® Commission

This will be included in the lawyer's statement of adjustments and is charged at closing. This amount can vary between 5-7% + HST of the sale price of the home. From this amount, the buyer's REALTOR® and your selling REALTOR® are paid.

Conclusion

I am writing this conclusion while on a solo vacay in Cuba. I decided to take this trip while in the middle of a heavy divorce process with my second husband. I thought that going alone would empower me and give me the opportunity to venture around this great little island like the freedom-seeking monkey that I am. Well, I'm bored senseless! Couples frolicking about, no one seems to speak English, and the Internet has been down since I got here. The staff has been aggressive with hitting on me, and it's not flattering – it's creepy. I am on day-three of overcast skies and rain...and I've been here three days. Do the math. This bites.

But do you know what doesn't bite? Making my own choices, right or wrong. Despite several women's movements over decades, we still find ourselves looking towards others to accomplish our goals, for acceptance, and to point us in the right direction. But we don't have to be perfect in every decision, ladies. We are allowed to turn to ourselves to make choices, and we are allowed to make mistakes. We learn from our mistakes. Bad choices wouldn't turn into good ones if there was never a consequence. Embrace your ability to choose while you can, because one day your choices may be very remote or non-existent. Live your life for the woman you have chosen to be; not the one everyone wants you to be. By accepting YOU, others will be drawn to your happiness and wisdom.

Being in a situation that doesn't serve you well can not only rob you of years of joy, it can detract from your health, money, and employment success, as well as your relationships with your children, siblings, and parents. When you make your own decisions, you have decided, for whatever reason of your own, to make a change in your life, whether it be planned or not, good or bad.

You have acquired my book, because you are a woman who wants to know more; a woman in charge of her life. This is not to say that a man can't feel just as empowered...but I didn't write this book for your ex, your deceased husband, your brother, or your father. I wrote this for you. You are special and so is the content herein – for a woman by a woman.

If you have had any benefit from my work please forward it to a friend, co-worker, or family member in need. It won't matter if this book has been mangled and well-loved. It is the gesture of one woman helping another in need that counts. Pass this on, or buy a new one. The latter buys me another lunch.

Now get out there girlfriend... embrace and celebrate your next chapter. You are a wonderful creature in all your tears and glory.

Sincerely, **Christine Denty**

not intended to solicit those under contract

Appendix (Home Inspection)

ASAP Home Inspections
Home Inspection Report

ASAP HOME INSPECTIONS & ENVIRONMENTAL TESTING

Inspection Address, Your Town, Ontario, H0H0H0

Inspection prepared for: John Smith
Date of Inspection: 22/4/2014 Time: 1700
Age of Home: approx 20-30 years Size: 2000-2500

Inspector: Jim Van Loosen
Certified Master Inspector
211 Stevenson Rd N, Oshawa, Ontario L1J5M7
Phone: 905-410-6717
Email: jim@asaphi.ca
www.asaphi.ca

Christine Denty

ASAP Home Inspections — Inspection Address, Your Town, Ontario

Report Summary

Exterior			
Page 5 Item: 7	Foundation Conditions	• Evidence of repair noted. The inspector cannot make any comment on the effectiveness of these repairs. Buyer should consult with seller if further information is required.	
Page 6 Item: 9	Window/Frame Conditions	• Minor wood softening noted. Recommend ongoing maintenance.	
Page 7 Item: 10	Stair Condition	• Missing guardrails observed. This is a "Safety Concern." Although guardrails may not have been required when the home was built, we recommend client consider installing guardrails as a safety enhancement. • Whenever three or more stairs are present a handrail is usually required.	
Page 9 Item: 15	Exterior Faucet Conditions	• Leaks at tap	
Garage			
Page 15 Item: 16	Garage Comments	• Stairs are very steep.	
Basement			
Page 16 Item: 3	Basement Stairs Condition	• Whenever three or more stairs are present a handrail is usually required.	
Page 17 Item: 4	Basement Floor Condition	• Floor drain observed but covered with carpet. This creates a potential trip hazard.	
Page 17 Item: 5	Basement Walls Condition	• Cracks and deterioration observed.	
Heating			
Page 23 Item: 7	Distribution Ducting Condition	• Highly recommend cleaning of ducts due to high amounts of dust in the home near registers.	
Water Heater			
Page 25 Item: 2	Supply lines Condition	• Corrosion noted at fittings.	
Kitchen			
Page 28 Item: 10	Kitchen Faucets	• Faucet is loose.	
Page 29 Item: 17	Microwave	• Microwave is loose. This may be caused by the screws being too tight and pulling the unit off the bracket at the back	
Bedrooms			

not intended to solicit those under contract

139

Page 30 Item: 5	Window Condition		• Fog/condensation observed in Thermopane windows. This is an indication of a failed seal. Recommend review for repair or replacement as necessary.
Bathrooms			
Page 32 Item: 4	Bathroom Ceiling Condition		• Evidence of past water penetration observed.
Page 33 Item: 7	Electrical Condition		• No GFCI protection present in basement bathroom, suggest installing GFCI protected receptacles for safety.
Page 34 Item: 9	Bathroom Exhaust Fan Condition		• Exhaust fan is noisy. and seizing
Page 34 Item: 11	Tub Surround Condition		• Suggest all tile edges and tub/shower walls be caulked and sealed to prevent moisture penetration. All missing/damaged grouting should be replaced. Failure to keep walls sealed can cause deterioration and extensive moisture damage to the interior walls and surrounding sub-flooring. This damage is not always visible or accessible to the inspector at the time of inspection.
Other Interior Areas			
Page 39 Item: 4	Door Conditions		• Door is taped at bottom on front storm door. This may indicate that the lower trim falls off.
Attic			
Page 41 Item: 4	Evidence of leaking		• Evidence of prior leaks observed
Page 43 Item: 10	Attic Comments		• Recommend caulking and installation of fresh weatherstripping at attic hatch to reduce build up of warm moist air.

Christine Denty

General Information

1. Inspector
Jim Van Loosen Certified Master Inspector

2. Persons in Attendance
Buyers • Buyers Agent • Buyer represented by agent. Inspection Agreement reviewed and signed by buyer/agent prior to inspection.

3. Occupancy
The Property is occupied

4. Property Information

5. Levels
2 Story

6. Estimated Age
This structure is approximately 20 to 30 years of age as stated by the agent.

7. Weather conditions
Cloudy • Cool • Rain today/recently • Temperature at the time of inspection was approximately 10 degrees. • Windy

Exterior

1. Driveway Condition
Materials: Asphalt
Observations:
- Suggest sealing to preserve the remaining life of the driveway.

2. Electric Meter Condition
Location: Right Side

3. Gas Meter Condition
Location: Left Side
Observations:
- Main fuel shutoff was located at the meter.

4. Walkway Conditions
Materials: Paver/Tile • Stone

not intended to solicit those under contract   141

5. Lot Grade and Drainage Conditions

Observations:
- Adding dirt backfill to any low lying areas located around the foundation is recommended to ensure proper drainage away from the foundation at all times.
- Flat Lot
- Re-grading where needed is recommended to assure all water drains away from the homes foundation at all times.

6. Exterior Wall Cladding Condition

Materials: Brick
Observations:
- Common cracks noted.

7. Foundation Conditions

Type: Basement
Observations:

- Concrete.
- Minor vertical cracking was noted. This cracking appeared typical of cracking that results during the curing process. Such "shrinkage cracks" are very common and are usually harmless. Should this cracking appear to worsen, consultation with a qualified contractor for required repairs is recommended.
- **Evidence of repair noted. The inspector cannot make any comment on the effectiveness of these repairs. Buyer should consult with seller if further information is required.**

8. Gutter Condition
Materials: Metal
Observations:
- Evidence of overflow observed.

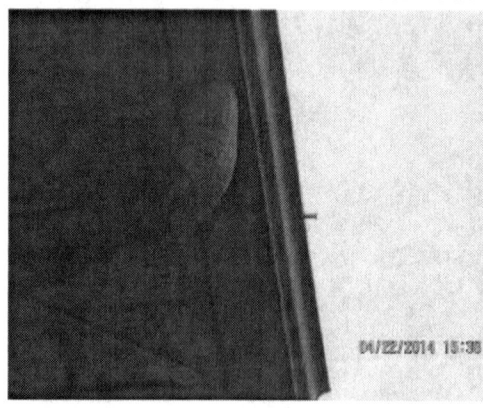

9. Window/Frame Conditions
Materials: Sliding Frame • Wood Frame
Observations:
- Peeling paint observed, suggest scraping and painting as necessary.
- Suggest caulking around doors and windows as necessary.
- Minor wood softening noted. Recommend ongoing maintenance.

10. Stair Condition

Observations:
- Missing guardrails observed. This is a "Safety Concern." Although guardrails may not have been required when the home was built, we recommend client consider installing guardrails as a safety enhancement.
- Whenever three or more stairs are present a handrail is usually required.

11. Porch Condition

Materials: Brick
Observations:
- No access to review of structural assembly.
- Recommend review by a qualified professional for repair or replacement as necessary.
- Settling observed.

12. Door Bell Condition
Location: Front

13. Electrical Conditions
Observations:
• Ground Fault Circuit Interrupters (GFCI) were not required when the home was built. Suggest client consider upgrading with GFCI's at all receptacles near water sources, such as the kitchen, the bathrooms, the garage, and exterior receptacles to enhance safety. Upgrades should be performed by a licensed electrician.

14. Exterior Door Conditions
Materials: Metal Clad • Metal Storm Door

15. Exterior Faucet Conditions
Location: Rear • Right Side
Observations:
- Check valve in place to prevent water backflow.
- Leaks at tap

16. Trim Conditions
Materials: Vinyl and Metal • Wood
Observations:
- Moisture damage, wood rot, observed. Recommend review for repair as necessary.

17. Fence Condition
Materials: Wood
Observations:
- Fence leaning in areas.
- Gate is sagging.
- Gate sticks.

18. Retaining Wall Conditions

19. Patio Conditions
Materials: Brick
Observations:
- Evidence of ponding observed.

20. Deck Condition

21. Balcony Condition

22. General Exterior Comments

Observations:
- An effective water management program is required for all homes. This includes maintenance of all wooden components, caulking of all openings and ongoing vigilance of water handling systems, roof and flashing. Buyer is advised that while there may not be evidence of water intrusion into structure at time of inspection, NO STATEMENT referring to future performance can be made due to changing weather and structure conditions.
- Barn/shed/outbuilding observed but not inspected.
- No window well covers observed, suggest installing well covers to keep out debris and for safety. Wells should be cleaned regularly for proper drainage.
- Suggest trimming back vegetation for proper clearance and ventilation.
- Above ground pool observed. Not inspected because it is still winterized.

Roof

1. Methods Used to Inspect Roof

How Inspected: Observed from the ground with 8X56 field glasses • Roof was visually inspected from accessible points on the interior and/or exterior. If a roof is too high, is too steep, is wet, or is composed of materials that can be damaged if walked upon, the roof is not mounted. Therefore, client is advised that this is a limited review and a licensed roofer should be contacted if a more detailed report is desired. • Visually accessible from ground. Not mounted due to wet surface.

2. Roof Condition

Materials: Asphalt Composition Shingles

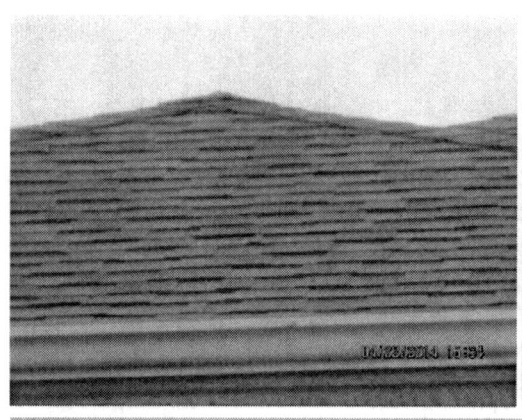

3. Roof Flashing Condition
Materials: Metal
Observations:
- Recommend resealing all flashings and through the roof vents as a part of routine maintenance.

4. Skylight Condition

5. Roof Surface Conditions
Observations:
- Relatively recent installation.
- The roof shows normal wear for its age and type.

6. Roof Comments

Observations:
- Roof appeared functional at time of inspection. No prediction of future performance or warranties can be offered.

Garage

1. Garage Type
Type: Attached

2. Garage Roof Condition
Observations:
- Same as house

3. Garage Exterior Conditions
Materials: Same as House

4. Gutter/ Downspout Conditions
Materials: Same as house

5. Garage Floor Condition
Materials: Concrete
Observations:
- Common cracks noted.
- Dry at the time of the inspection.
- Efflorescence observed; this is a mineral deposit left behind from exterior water infiltration.

6. Garage Door Condition
Materials: Roll-up Panel
Observations:
- Peeling paint observed, suggest painting or staining, as necessary, to preserve the remaining life of the door.

| ASAP Home Inspections | Inspection Address, Your Town, Ontario |

7. Garage Door Hardware Condition

8. Garage Door Opener Condition

9. Garage Window Conditions

10. Exterior Door Condition

11. Fire Door Conditions
Materials: Metal/Metal Clad
Observations:
- Self closer installed as a safety feature.

12. Fire Wall Condition

13. Garage Wall Condition
Materials: Drywall • Unfinished
Observations:
- Dry at the time of the inspection.

14. Garage Ceiling Condition
Materials: Drywall
Observations:
- Dry at the time of the inspection.

15. Garage Electrical Condition

Observations:
- No GFCI protection present, suggest installing GFCI protected receptacles for safety.

16. Garage Comments

Observations:
- Stairs are very steep.

Chimney

1. Chimney Comments

2. Chimney Condition

3. Flue Condition

4. Flashing Conditions

5. Spark Arrester/Rain Cap Condition

6. Chimney Comments

Basement

1. Basement Access

Basement stairway.

2. Foundation Comments

Type: Basement • Finished Basement
Observations:
- Finished basement: finished areas in basement were observed. Access to the original basement walls, floors, and ceilings was not available due to the additional construction that is present such as framed out walls, covered ceilings, and added floor coverings. As these areas are not visible or accessible to the inspector they are excluded from this inspection.
- Inaccessible areas behind walls, ceiling and floor coverings are not within the scope of this report. Buyer is urged to review the Seller's Property Information Sheet to determine if any issues such as seepage have occurred in past as this inspection is limited to visually accessible items only.
- Limited view due to storage of personal property.

3. Basement Stairs Condition

Observations:
- No light observed, suggest installing a light fixture in hallway at bottom of stairway for safety.
- **Whenever three or more stairs are present a handrail is usually required.**

4. Basement Floor Condition

Materials: Carpet
Observations:
- All concrete floor slabs experience some degree of cracking due to shrinkage in the drying process. In most instances floor coverings prevent recognition of cracks or settlement in all but the most severe cases. Where carpeting and other floor coverings are installed, the materials and condition of the flooring underneath cannot be determined.
- Floor drain observed but covered with carpet. This creates a potential trip hazard.

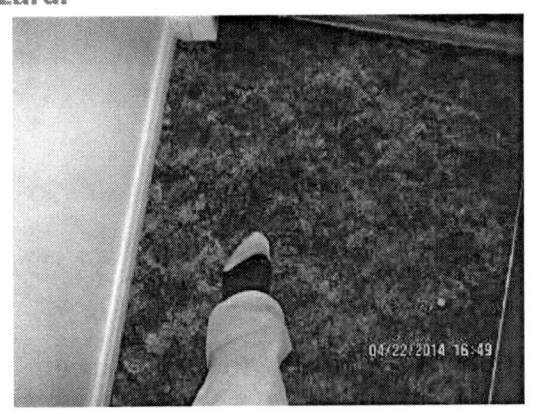

5. Basement Walls Condition

Materials: Drywall
Observations:
- Dry at the time of the inspection.
- Cracks and deterioration observed.

6. Basement Ceilings Condition

Materials: Drywall • Unfinished
Observations:
- Dry at the time of the inspection.
- Evidence of past water penetration observed in cold cellar

| ASAP Home Inspections | Inspection Address, Your Town, Ontario |

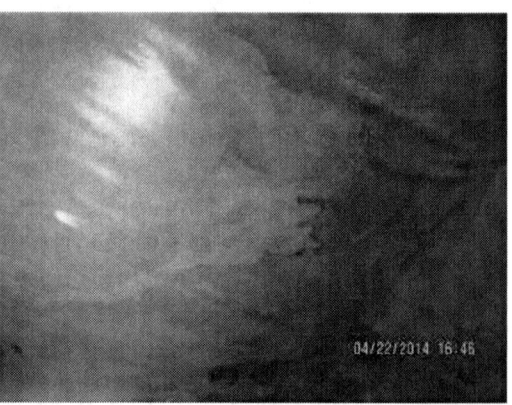

7. Exterior Doors Condition

8. Joist Condition
Materials: Conventional 2 x 10 Framing

9. Beams Condition
Materials: Metal
Observations:
- Beams are partially finished, unable to fully inspect.

10. Support Post Comments
Materials: Metal
Observations:
- Posts are partially finished, unable to fully inspect.

11. Subfloor Condition
Materials: Wafer Board
Observations:
- No leaks were observed at the time of the inspection.

12. Window Condition
Style: Sliding Frame • Steel Frame

13. Electrical Conditions
Observations:
- Reversed polarity observed, recommend review for repair as necessary.

14. Visible Plumbing Condition
Materials: ABS • Copper

15. Insulation Condition
Materials: Fiberglas
Observations:
- Visible at unfinished area only

16. Distribution/Ducts
Ducts/Registers
Observations:
- Very limited review of ductwork due to basement finish.

17. Basement Comments
Observations:
- Limited review due to finished basement. Recommend client refer to the Seller Disclosure Statement regarding the condition of any concealed plumbing and foundation elements.
- Buyer is advised to refer to Disclosure Statement regarding past water intrusion if any.
- Limited review due to storage of personal property.
- Recommend client refer to the Seller Disclosure Statement regarding the condition of any concealed plumbing and foundation elements.
- The presence of mold in concealed areas of the home does NOT fall within the scope of Home Inspection as it is not visibly accessible. If buyer has concerns about mold due to allergies, or suspects the presence of mold, he/she is advised to consult with a qualified contractor and with vendor to agree to carry out destructive investigation. Ie. Opening walls to search for sources of an issue.

Plumbing

1. Main Shutoff Location
Materials: Copper • Public supply
Observations:
- Basement wall hatch.
- Since main shutoff valves are operated infrequently, it is not unusual for them to become frozen over time. They often leak or break when operated after a period of inactivity. For this reason main shutoff valves are not tested during a home inspection. We suggest caution when operating shutoffs that have not been turned for a long period of time. All shutoff valves and angle stops should be turned regularly to ensure free movement in case of emergency.

2. Supply Line Condition
Materials: Copper

3. Waste Line Conditions
Materials: Public Waste
Observations:
- Municipal waste.

4. Waste Line Condition
Materials: ABS
Observations:
- No leaks observed at the time of the inspection.
- Limited inspection of waste lines due to basement finish

5. Sump Pump Conditions

6. Sump Pump Plumbing

7. Sump Pit Conditions

8. Ejector Pump Conditions

9. Venting Conditions

10. Plumbing Comments
Comments:
- All plumbing components tested well at time of inspection unless otherwise noted.

Electrical

1. Main Service Drop Condition
Type: Main Service Drop is underground

2. Electrical panel Condition
Type / Materials: Breakers • Branch circuit wiring is copper
Observations:
- Overload protection provided by breakers.
- Main disconnects are present.
- Open positions observed for future expansion.
- The main service is approximately 100 amps, 240 volts.

3. Main Panel Comments

Observations:
- Improper clearance access to areas around the panel. Recommend enlarging the hole for easier access.

4. Sub Panel Comments

5. Smoke detector comments

Location: Basement • Main Floor • Second Floor
Observations:
- Periodic testing is suggested to ensure proper working order.
- Suggest installing additional smoke detectors in appropriate areas as needed to enhance fire safety. Periodic testing is suggested to ensure proper working order and to enhance fire safety.
- While there may be serviceable smoke and carbon monoxide detectors in the house at time of inspection, buyer is urged to review existence of such upon close as they are on occasion removed by seller. These items are generally mandatory in all municipalities.

6. Electrical Comments

Observations:
- Reversed polarity, hot and neutral reversed and other terms used for electric receptacles are usually easily corrected by minor wiring adjustments at the specified item. When these conditions are noted in this report, a licensed electrician should be consulted for repairs/replacement as needed to ensure safety.

Heating

1. Heating
Type: Gas Forced Air

2. Burner Chamber Comments
Observations:
- Annual service is recommended.
- No record of recent service observed.
- Partially Visible

3. Exhaust Venting Conditions
Materials: Plastic

4. Humidifier Comments

5. Air Filter Condition
Observations:
- We recommend changing or cleaning the filter monthly during the heating season.

6. Thermostat Condition
Located at the living room

7. Distribution Ducting Condition
Type: Ducts and Registers
Observations:
- No leaks were observed at the time of the inspection.
- Highly recommend cleaning of ducts due to high amounts of dust in the home near registers.

8. Heating Comments

Observations:
- Due to the higher efficiency of this unit, this review is limited. Most areas are sealed and inaccessible. We suggest review by a licensed heating contractor if a more detailed review is desired.
- This was a very limited inspection as inspector is neither qualified nor authorized to carry out a technically exhaustive inspection of heating system. Buyer is advised to have this system serviced annually to ensure safe and efficient operation.

Carbon monoxide detectors are mandatory in most municipalities and should be installed in furnace area and bedroom area at minimum.

- Unable to inspect heat exchanger due to closed system.

Air Conditioning

The heating, ventilation, and air conditioning and cooling system (often referred to as HVAC) is the climate control system for the structure. The goal of these systems is to keep the occupants at a comfortable level while maintaining indoor air quality, ventilation while keeping maintenance costs at a minimum. The HVAC system is usually powered by electricity and natural gas, but can also be powered by other sources such as butane, oil, propane, solar panels, or wood.

The inspector will usually test the heating and air conditioner using the thermostat or other controls. For a more thorough investigation of the system please contact a licensed HVAC service person.

1. Air Conditioning Comments

Type: Electric • Split System
Observations:
- Air conditioning could not be inspected as system was still closed down by owner. Activating air conditioning during cool/cold weather or without seasonal preparation can cause serious damage to the system. Buyer is advised to verify satisfactory operation prior to close.
- Electrical disconnect provided near this unit for safety.
- Electrical service must be re-established 48 hours prior to operating this unit.

Christine Denty

Water Heater

1. Water Heater

2. Supply lines Condition

Materials: Copper
Observations:

- Gas shut off valve was observed near this appliance.
- Ground bond wire noted from gas line to copper supply line over water heater. This is a vital component to over all grounding of house.
- **Corrosion noted at fittings.**

3. Temperature Pressure Release Valve Conditions

ASAP Home Inspections	Inspection Address, Your Town, Ontario

4. Combustion Chamber Conditions
Observations:
- Inaccessible

5. Flue Venting Conditions
Materials: Plastic
Observations:
- Intact where visible; the flue interior was not reviewed.

6. Water Heater Comments
Observations:
- Children should be kept away from water heater as the high pressure release valve, if disturbed, can cause scalding.

Kitchen
The kitchen is used for food preparation and often for entertainment. Kitchens typically include a stove, dishwasher, sink and other appliances.

1. Kitchen Floor Condition
Materials: Wood
Observations:
- Minor damage noted.

2. Kitchen Walls Condition
Materials: Drywall/Plaster
Observations:
- Dry at the time of the inspection.
- No stains or evidence of moisture penetration observed.

3. Ceiling Conditions
Materials: Drywall/Plaster
Observations:
- Dry at the time of the inspection.

4. Kitchen Doors Condition

5. Kitchen Windows Condition

6. Kitchen Electrical Condition

Observations:
- GFCI protected receptacles may not have been required when the house was built. We suggest buyer consider upgrading with GFCI's at all receptacles near water sources.

7. Kitchen Cabinet Condition

Observations:
- Doors are out of alignment.

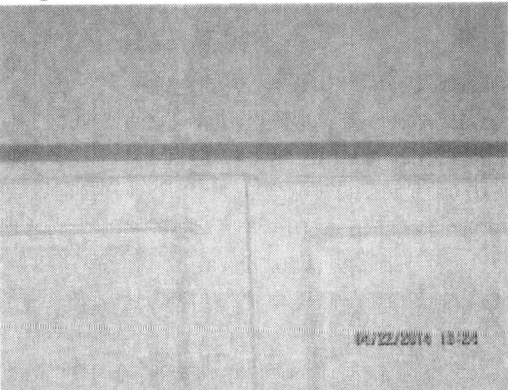

8. Kitchen Counter Top Condition

Observations:
- Minor damage noted.

9. Kitchen Sink Condition

Materials: Fiberglas
Observations:
- Sink is loose, suggest securing as necessary.

10. Kitchen Faucets

Observations:
- **Faucet is loose.**

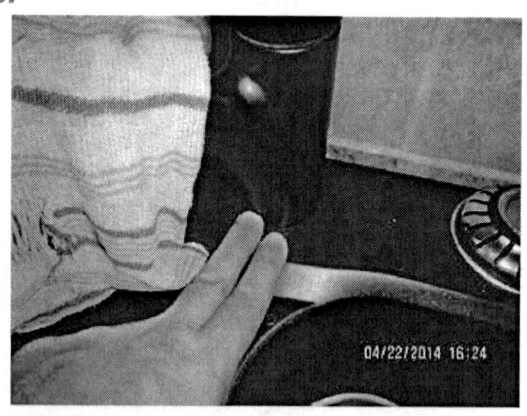

11. Traps/Drains/Supply Condition

Observations:
- No way to determine presence of trap under sink as it is (if present) concealed between subfloor and ceiling finish.

12. Stove Cooktop Conditions

Style: Electric
Observations:
- Electric elements may fail without warning
- Recommend confirming proper operation prior to close.
- The electrical stove/range elements were tested at the time of inspection and appeared to function properly. These can fail at anytime without warning. No warranty, guarantee, or certification is given as to future failure.

13. Oven Conditions

Style: Electric
Observations:
- Electric elements may fail without warning
- Recommend confirming proper operation prior to close.
- The upper and lower electric oven elements were tested at the time of inspection and appeared to function properly. These can fail at anytime without warning. No warranty, guarantee, or certification is given as to future failures.

14. Garbage Disposal

15. Dishwasher Condition
Observations:
- Dishwasher operating upon arrival of inspector. Buyer is advised that no warranty is offered on this or any other appliance, as outlined in Inspection Agreement.

16. Hood Fan Condition
Exterior Vented
Observations:
- Central ventilation system is present.

17. Microwave
Observations:
- **Microwave is loose. This may be caused by the screws being too tight and pulling the unit off the bracket at the back**

18. Kitchen Comments

The main area of inspection in the bedrooms is the structural system. This means that all walls, ceilings and floors will be inspected. Doors and windows will also be investigated for damage and normal operation. Personal items in the bedroom may prevent all areas to be inspected as the inspector will not move personal items.

Bedrooms

1. Floor Condition
Observations:
- Minor damage noted.

2. Wall Condition

Observations:
- Dry at the time of the inspection.
- No stains or evidence of moisture penetration observed.
- Nail pops noted.

3. Ceiling Conditions

Observations:
- Dry at the time of the inspection.
- No stains or evidence of moisture penetration observed.

4. Door Conditions

5. Window Condition

Observations:
- Apparent mold and debris on window frames noted. This may indicate moisture issues such as frost on windows.
- **Fog/condensation observed in Thermopane windows. This is an indication of a failed seal. Recommend review for repair or replacement as necessary.**

6. Electrical Conditions

7. Stair Conditions

| ASAP Home Inspections | Inspection Address, Your Town, Ontario |

8. Other Interior Area Comments

Observations:
- Evidence of truss uplift at various areas. This is a relatively common condition and is normally not a serious concern. Recommend consultation with qualified contractor for repairs if condition worsens.
- Minor cosmetic issues are not within the scope of this inspection as it focuses on basic structure and major systems only.
- Recently painted walls and ceilings can conceal previous and current water issues. No moisture readings noted at time of inspection.
- This inspection report recognizes the fact that this property is suffering from some deferred maintenance and is in need of updating in a number of areas. With this in mind we have purposefully overlooked things such as worn flooring and stuck or sticking doors and windows. The main intention of this report is to identify major operational defects and areas of necessary maintenance.

Bathrooms

Bathrooms can consist of many features from Jacuzzi tubs and showers to toilets and bidets. Because of all the plumbing involved it is an important area of the house to look over. Moisture in the air and leaks can cause mildew, wallpaper and paint to peel, and other problems. The home inspector will identify as many issues as possible but some problems may be undetectable due to problems within the walls or under the flooring..

1. Bathroom Location

Location: Basement • Main Floor • Second Floor Common Bathroom • Ensuite to Master bedroom

2. Bath Floor Conditions

Materials: Ceramic Tile • Linoleum
Observations:
- Minor damage noted.

3. Bathroom Wall Condition

Materials: Drywall/Plaster
Observations:
- Dry at the time of the inspection.
- No stains or evidence of moisture penetration observed.

4. Bathroom Ceiling Condition

Materials: Drywall/Plaster
Observations:
- Evidence of past water penetration observed.

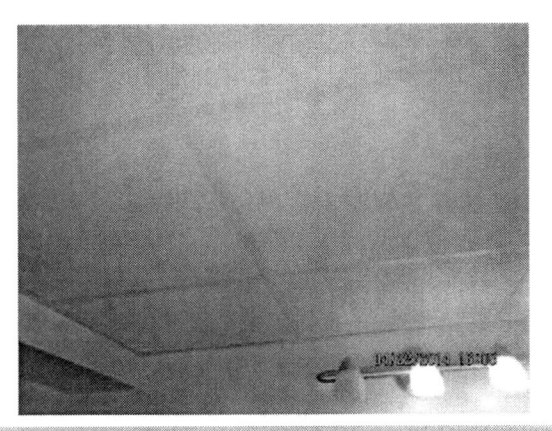

5. Bathroom Doors Condition
Materials: Hollow Core

6. Bathroom Windows Condition

7. Electrical Condition
Observations:
• **No GFCI protection present in basement bathroom, suggest installing GFCI protected receptacles for safety.**

8. Heat Source Condition
Type: Central Heating and Cooling

9. Bathroom Exhaust Fan Condition
Observations:
- Central ventilation is present.
- Exhaust fan is noisy, and seizing

10. Tub/Whirlpool Condition
Style: Tub

11. Tub Surround Condition
Materials: Ceramic Tile
Observations:
- **Suggest all tile edges and tub/shower walls be caulked and sealed to prevent moisture penetration. All missing/damaged grouting should be replaced. Failure to keep walls sealed can cause deterioration and extensive moisture damage to the interior walls and surrounding sub-flooring. This damage is not always visible or accessible to the inspector at the time of inspection.**

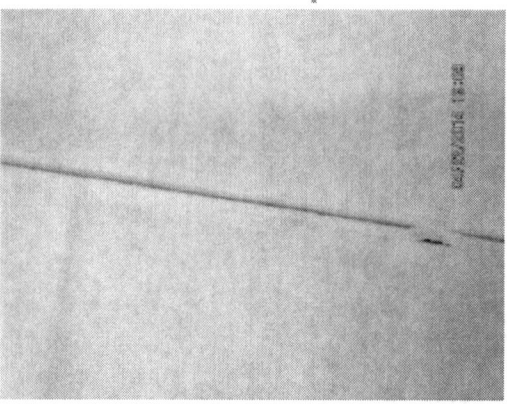

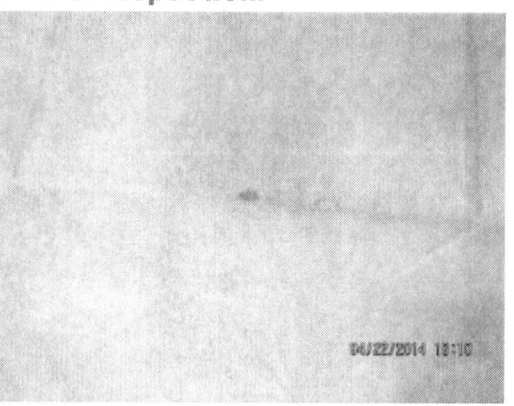

12. Tub Enclosure Condition

13. Tub Faucet Condition

14. Shower Base Condition
Materials: Fiberglas
Observations:
• Evidence of damage and repairs. The inspector cannot comment on the effectiveness of these repairs.

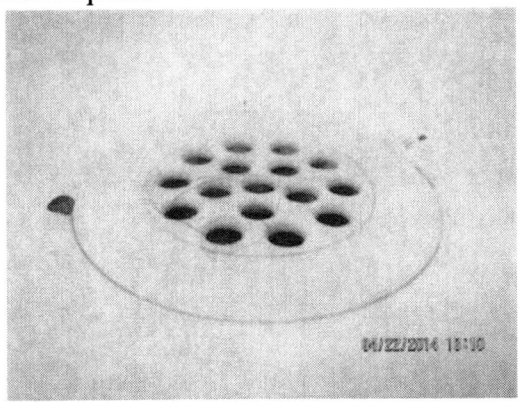

15. Shower Surround Condition
Materials: Fiberglass
Observations:
• Suggest all tile edges and tub/shower walls be caulked and sealed to prevent moisture penetration. All missing/damaged grouting should be replaced. Failure to keep walls sealed can cause deterioration and extensive moisture damage to the interior walls and surrounding sub-flooring. This damage is not always visible or accessible to the inspector at the time of inspection.

16. Shower Door Condition
Materials: Tempered Safety Glass

17. Shower Faucet Condition

18. Sink Condition
Materials: Metal

| ASAP Home Inspections | Inspection Address, Your Town, Ontario |

19. Sink Faucet Condition

20. Traps/Drains/Supply Condition

21. Toilet Condition

22. Bidet Condition

23. Counters/Cabinets Condition

Observations:
- Suggest caulking as necessary.
- Minor damage noted.

24. Steamer Condition

25. Bathroom Comments

Laundry Area

1. Laundry Area Location

Location: Main Floor

2. Floors
Materials: Linoleum
Observations:
- Minor damage noted.

3. Walls Condition
Materials: Drywall/Plaster
Observations:
- Dry at the time of the inspection.
- No stains or evidence of moisture penetration observed.

4. Ceiling Condition
Materials: Drywall/Plaster
Observations:
- Dry at the time of the inspection.

5. Door Condition
Materials: Hollow Core

6. Window Condition
Materials: Sliding Frame

7. Cabinet Condition
Observations:
- Minor damage noted.

8. Laundry Tub/Sink Condition
Materials: Plastic

9. Laundry Faucets

10. Electrical Conditions
Observations:
- GFCI protected receptacles may not have been required when the house was built. We suggest buyer consider upgrading with GFCI's at all receptacles near water sources.

11. Washer Hook-ups
Observations:
- Washer drains into sink drain. Recommend separate standpipe to prevent flooding if using these faucets in the sink.

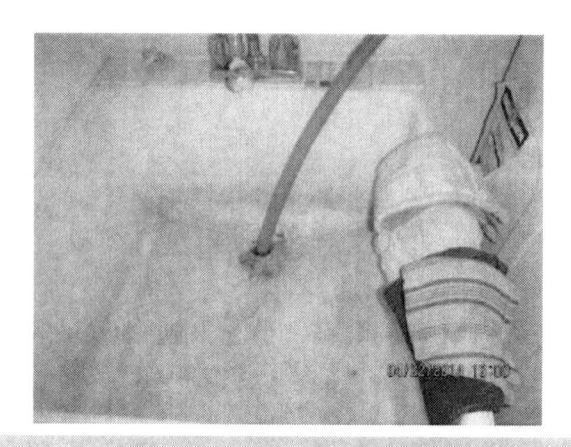

12. Dryer Hook-ups
Observations:
- Electric
- Dryer is not properly vented, suggest metal vent to the exterior.

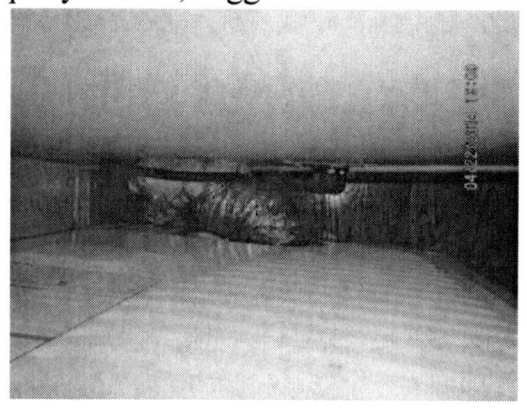

13. Exhaust Fan Condition
Observations:
- None observed, we recommend an exhaust fan be installed in all bathrooms for proper ventilation and moisture control.

14. Laundry Comments
Observations:
- This is a limited review due to storage of personal property.

Other Interior Areas
The Interior section covers areas of the house that are not considered part of the Bathrooms, Bedrooms, Kitchen or areas covered elsewhere in the report. Interior areas usually consist of

hallways, foyer, and other open areas. Within these areas the inspector is performing a visual inspection and will report visible damage, wear and tear, and moisture problems if seen. Personal items in the structure may prevent the inspector from viewing all areas on the interior.

The inspector does not usually test for mold or other hazardous materials. A qualified expert should be consulted if you would like further testing.

1. Floor Condition

Observations:
- Minor damage noted.

2. Wall Condition

Observations:
- Dry at the time of the inspection.
- No stains or evidence of moisture penetration observed.
- Patching observed.

3. Ceiling Conditions

Observations:
- Dry at the time of the inspection.
- No stains or evidence of moisture penetration observed.

4. Door Conditions

Observations:
- Door is taped at bottom on front storm door. This may indicate that the lower trim falls off.

5. Window Condition

Observations:
- Deterioration of wooden frames noted. While basic maintenance may prolong the life of these window frames, replacement may be necessary at some point.
- Peeling paint observed, suggest scraping and painting as necessary.

6. Electrical Conditions

7. Wet Bar Conditions

8. Stair Conditions

9. Other Interior Area Comments

Observations:
- Compliance of basement apartments does not fall within the scope of Home Inspection. Should Municipal Compliance be a concern to buyer, he/she is advised to consult with the local authorities.
- Minor cosmetic issues are not within the scope of this inspection as it focuses on basic structure and major systems only.
- Recently painted walls and ceilings can conceal previous and current water issues. No moisture readings noted at time of inspection.
- This inspection report recognizes the fact that this property is suffering from some deferred maintenance and is in need of updating in a number of areas. With this in mind we have purposefully overlooked things such as worn flooring and stuck or sticking doors and windows. The main intention of this report is to identify major operational defects and areas of necessary maintenance.

Attic

1. Methods Used to Inspect
How Inspected: Accessible

2. Framing Condition
Style: Truss
Observations:
- Limited review due to insulation installed between the rafters.

3. Sheathing Condition

Materials: Plywood
Observations:
- Minor staining at nail penetrations. This is typical and expected for roofs of this age and conditions. Recommend monitoring. No predictions can be made relative to water intrusion due to changing conditions.

4. Evidence of leaking

Observations:
- Dry at the time of the inspection.
- Moisture stains at nails observed, which is an indication of inadequate ventilation.
- **Evidence of prior leaks observed**

5. Insulation Condition

Materials: Fiberglass • Loose Fill Insulation
Observations:
- 10-12" of insulation present.
- Insulation is blocking soffit vents, recommend clearing vents for proper ventilation.
- Recommend removing insulation for proper ventilation of the roof deck.

ASAP Home Inspections · Inspection Address, Your Town, Ontario

6. Ventilation Conditions

Style: Hooded Roof Vents • Soffit Vents
Observations:

- Soffit vents are blocked with insulation.

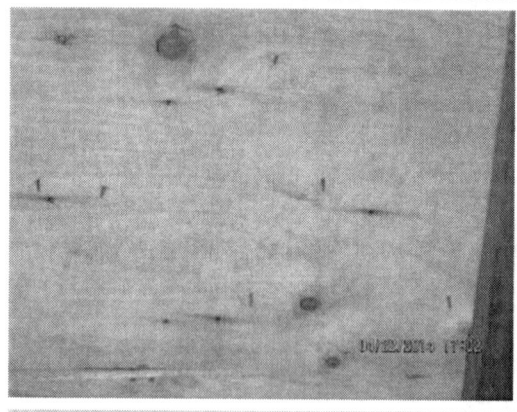

7. Window Conditions

8. Electrical Conditions

9. Distribution/Ducting Conditions

10. Attic Comments

Observations:
- Attic should be reviewed at least twice per year to ensure ventilation openings are clear and to ensure development of mould is kept in check. While there may be very little or no evidence of mould build-up in the attic at time of inspection, it can reproduce and spread rapidly should conditions allow it to. Mould can be potentially hazardous and will spread when moisture enters the attic cavity and is not vented to the exterior. Any area of suspected mould should be reviewed by a qualified contractor for analysis and removal.
- Recommend caulking and installation of fresh weatherstripping at attic hatch to reduce build up of warm moist air.

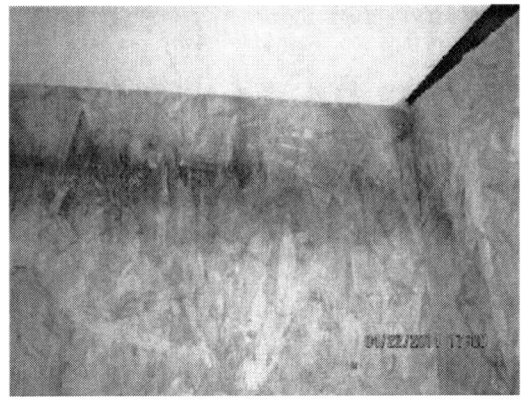

Fireplace

1. Fireplace Location
Location: Dining area

2. Fireplace Style
Style: Gas Direct vent. It can only be assumed that this appliance was installed to manufacturer's specifications.

3. Fireplace Comments
Observations:
- Pilot light "off" at time of inspection. Lighting of pilot lights is not within the scope of inspection. Buyer is therefore urged to ensure satisfactory operation of this unit prior to close.

| ASAP Home Inspections | Inspection Address, Your Town, Ontario |

Crawlspace

1. Crawlspace Access

2. Foundation Comments

3. Crawlspace Stairs Condition

4. Crawlspace Floor Condition

5. Crawlspace Walls Condition

6. Crawlspace Ceilings Condition

7. Exterior Doors Condition

8. Joist Condition

9. Beams Condition

ASAP Home Inspections — Inspection Address, Your Town, Ontario

10. Support Post Comments

11. Subfloor Condition

12. Window Condition

13. Ventilation Comments

14. Electrical Conditions

15. Visible Plumbing Condition

16. Insulation Condition

17. Distribution/Ducts

18. Vapor Barrier

19. Crawlspace Comments